Rik Mayall
—*is*—
THE·NEW STATESMAN

Rik Mayall
— *is* —
THE·NEW STATESMAN

ANNA MORGAN

JAVELIN BOOKS
LONDON · NEW YORK · SYDNEY

First published in the UK 1987 by Javelin Books, Artillery House, Artillery Row London SW1 1RT

Text copyright © 1987 ANNA MORGAN
Series copyright © 1987 YORKSHIRE TELEVISION LIMITED

Distributed in Australia by
Capricorn Link (Australia) Pty Ltd,
PO Box 665, Lane Cove, NSW 2066

[CIP Data]

ISBN 0 7137 2022 0

All rights reserved. No part of this book may be reproduced or transmitted in any form or by any means, electronic or mechanical, including photocopying, recording or any information storage and retrieval system, without permission in writing from the publisher.

This book is sold subject to the conditions that it shall not, by way of trade or otherwise, be lent, re-sold, hired out or otherwise circulated without the publisher's prior consent in any form of binding or cover other than that in which it is published and without a similar condition including this condition being imposed on the subsequent purchaser.

Typeset by Inforum Ltd, Portsmouth
Printed in Great Britain by
Cox & Wyman Ltd, Reading, Berks.

To Jason and Max

12 JUNE 1987

It's a pity about the other two, but those are the breaks of the game. It's a game called politics: it's a game called life.

When Mayor Cookson announced the results last night with 'Caslon, William Richard – Labour, Intensive Care – 3,237; Roper, Martin, Cyril – SDP, critical – 1,265; Sutch, Screaming Lord – Monster Raving Loony – 5,019; B'Stard, Alan Beresford – Conservative – 31,756 . . .', it was the fulfilment of my life's ambition.

Sarah, my wife, and Beatrice, my Agent, kissed each other in joy. I kissed and hugged them both triumphantly. Then I sobered, the weight of my new office already on my shoulders. As I raised my hand to quell the throng, silence descended like a stone.

'I should like to begin by thanking my loving wife Sarah, my Political Agent Beatrice Protheroe, and particularly the Chief Constable for East Yorkshire, Sir Malachi Jellicoe, who has made sure this election has been kept within the boundaries of the law,' I began, trying to appease that old fart who's been dogging my every step since that day Roper's Volvo found itself twisted round Caslon's Cortina, and whose rank breath I now felt searing the back of my neck as he wasted no time in coming forward to receive his share of the limelight. After a small smattering of applause, I continued, 'Unfortunately, my victory has been marred by the tragedy that has befallen two of my worthy opponents, so I ask you all to stand in silence for one minute.'

The hall stood in reverent rustling for a number of seconds while I wrestled with a smile that kept creeping up on me. Sir Malachi surreptitiously tapped me on the shoulder with a tattered cardboard file.

'I know why those cars crashed, B'Stard. And I know you know why those cars crashed,' he hissed malevolently.

How in God's name had that maniac found out about my little deal with Luigi, the 'Italian mechanic'? Still staring brightly at the hushed crowd, I whispered, 'How much do you want? Ten thousand? Twenty thousand?'

'Why do you assume I'm angling for a bribe?' Sir Malachi retorted sotto voce, flummoxing me.

'You can't arrest me here, now, during my finest moment,' I'm ashamed to say I pleaded.

'I'm not arresting you, B'Stard. You're far more use to me in Parliament than in prison,' he assured me.

'Of course I am, and if there's anything I can do for you – after all you're now one of my constituents.' My sigh of relief signalled the end of the hall's minute of silence.

'Yes, I am,' Sir Malachi remarked above the resumed celebrations. 'And there's a law I want passing,' he added in a sinister whisper. With that enigmatic hint, Sir Malachi left the stage.

This morning I awoke with the biggest majority in the House of Commons. The Honourable Member for Haltemprice gave his wife a good seeing to. One day soon I'll get my book published and make another fortune. Move over Jeffrey, here comes the best-selling *HOW TO BE A SIXTY-SECOND LOVER* by Alan Beresford B'Stard MP.

CHAPTER ONE

HAPPINESS IS A WARM GUN

It didn't take long for Sir Malachi Jellicoe to come to his point. In the few days before I took my seat he followed me round everywhere as I greeted my new constituents, a barmy presence in the first balmy week after the election. He kept flapping his dossier at me ominously, ranting on about arming the police.

I had to get the damning evidence of my file back, so I had to swear before God that I'd see that the police had might as well as right on their persons, and by the time I entered the Mother of Parliaments I'd managed to half-convince myself of the Chief Constable's case. In fact, I'd thought of one major argument in its favour: I could stand to make an enormous amount of boodle out of it.

Office space is very hard to find in the House, and I ended up in a cramped room on the top floor sharing with Sir Stephen Baxter, ancient member for E. Sussex, and Piers Fletcher-Dervish, Member for S. Wilts, whom I have in my pocket, though I must say a soiled hankie, three marbles, a conker and a copy of the *Beano* would be just as useful, especially right now. I'd had the tremendous good fortune to draw the ballot for a Private Member's Bill before the break. God was obviously on my side. I'd ranted myself hoarse, and in no time at all a Select Committee had been set up. We'd got to go on a couple of jollys to New York and Los Angeles, and the Bill went through after two readings. The mood of the House was just right, if you don't count those left-wing loonies who whinge on and on about any little thing and who now had to be swayed by my rhetoric. I was running out of ideas.

I tried the speech out on myself. 'We claim we are full and enthusiastic members of the European Community, yet we are the only member state whose police don't carry guns. So, how can they be expected to respond when heavily armed French bank robbers come swarming through the Channel Tunnel?'

'I say, Alan, that's awfully good,' Piers said.

'You like it?'

'Rather, I think it's wonderful,' Piers nodded.

'Then it must be rubbish,' I said, screwing up the paper and dropping it on to the floor.

'That speech is a bit of a problem, isn't it?' was Piers's lame commiseration.

I lost my temper. 'I can't understand why you're not in the Cabinet, Piers, with a razor-sharp brain like yours! Heaven only knows how you got elected! But then your constituency is south of Watford where a hatstand would get in if they put a blue rosette on it.' The phone ringing interrupted my newly found flow. I answered it with my usual 'Alan B'Stard, biggest majority in the House. . . .'

It was Sir Malachi. 'Yes, Sir Malachi, the vote's this afternoon. With a little luck you can be shooting suspects by teatime. Now, about that little road accident I had nothing to do with,' I lowered my voice. The Chief Constable hung up before I could remind him about my file.

At that moment my other stablemate, Sir Stephen Baxter, doddered in from lunch. Sir Stephen is a nice old boy who keeps telling me that he was once a wild young backbencher, but now has only one ambition. Maggie keeps wanting to kick him Upstairs but as he is seventy-six and there is only one Member older than himself, he's hanging on by a thread until they make him Father of the House. His only claim to fame was being an innocent victim of the *Profumo* Scandal, after Lord Denning wrote that it had been Sir Stephen whom Profumo had sent across to Timothy White's in Trafalgar Square for a packet of Durex Featherlite.

'Big day for you, B'Stard,' Sir Stephen said as he creaked his way to his desk. 'Third Reading of Your Private Member's Bill. . . .'

Smart as a whip, as usual. 'Oh, is it today? Good thing you reminded me. I was going to slope off at half-past two to visit a massage parlour.' Sir Stephen looked shocked. After a second or so he laughed. 'Very good! I know a joke when I hear one and I may have just heard one then!'

'Look, both of you, I'm trying to write a speech. Go away', I begged.

Sir Stephen lowered his voice and said to Piers, 'It's extraordinary really. B'Stard's only been in the House for three months and he's on the verge of arming the police.' I scowled him into silence. After a few seconds Piers broke it. 'Alan's got writer's block,' he whispered to Sir Stephen.

'Have you? Then why don't I give you a preview of my intended oration. Might get the creative juices flowing.' Sir Stephen cleared his throat and picked up his speech. 'For a century and a half, the brave British Bobby has patrolled the beat on his trusty bicycle, armed only with his sturdy truncheon, his whistle and his considerable courage,' Sir Stephen volunteered.

'Hear, hear!' Piers shouted.

'Old hat!' I snorted.

'Do you really think so? All right, armed with his whistle, his considerable courage and his old hat.'

I ask you.

After struggling for another half-hour with my speech, I discovered that Sir Stephen's wasn't that bad after all, so I stole it.

The long and short of it is that the speech was brilliant, especially with some subtle embellishments of my own that really won the day. I continued to read from Sir Stephen's speech for fifteen minutes or so, '. . . for this green and pleasant land, this bosky paradise, must not be forfeited to the Goths and the Vandals. Therefore our plucky Peelers need powerful pistols for their purpose and protection. As Wordsworth put it, "Who is this happy warrior? Who is he that every man in arms should wish to be?" '

This was too much, and losing the crowd. I threw away my notes and temporised, 'To hell with poetry. As far as I'm concerned, arming the police is simple common sense. So, in the immortal words of "Hill Street Blues", let's do it to them before they do it to us!'

That brought the House down. The Speaker called Mr Robert Crippen, a raving militant from my neighbouring constituency. I hate him.

'I speak against the Bill as a man who, on demonstration, picket line and sit-in, has often been on the receiving end of a brave bobby's sturdy truncheon. I now realise that a bullet in the brain would have put less strain on the National Health Service.'

'Hear, hear!' I shouted.

Crippen went on most unconvincingly, 'In my part of Yorkshire, the Chief Constable of the East Riding, Sir Malachi Jellicoe, already poses a major threat to civil liberties. He has recently organised public book burnings of volumes he deems blasphemous, obscene or both. So wide are his criteria that there are now only sixty-seven books left in the East Yorkshire Public Library System! Some call Sir Malachi a zealot: I call him a nutter. And if this Bill becomes law, this nutter will have a heavily armed force at his disposal, taking us one more step to a right-wing Tory police state.'

I leaped to my feet, 'Exactly the purpose of my bill!' I said, putting paid to Comrade Bob's further comments. Piers jumped up a second later saying, 'Exactly the purpose of his bill!' with more enthusiasm than intelligence.

After some confusion, Sir Stephen graciously forgave me for pinching his speech and using it for the betterment of mankind as we know it. While we shared a bottle of champagne in the office I tried to get through to the ravishing Beatrice, but she was out. So I 'phoned Sarah with the wonderful news.

'Yes, darling, it got through with a huge majority. Well, eleven,' I said truthfully. 'Would have been twelve but Piers got so excited during the debate that he spent the division in the loo.'

Sarah giggled and sighed, 'I miss you, darling. Wish you were here with me now.'

'That's politics, Fluffy Tail,' I murmured, feeling randy with my glowing success. 'By the way, I don't suppose you've heard from Beatrice Protheroe, have you?'

Sarah said she hadn't. 'Because she doesn't seem to be in London, and I need her to organise saturation media coverage for my magnificent triumph' – and boff speechless, I added to myself.

'If I see her, I'll tell her,' Sarah promised.

'All right, darling. Yearn for you longingly,' I whispered fondly.

'That's nice, darling. I'm your little rabbit.' We made rabbit noises at each other and hung up.

I drained my champagne glass and waved to the chaps. 'Right, I'm off to Stringfellows to commit adultery.' 'Can I come, too?' Piers asked hopefully. 'I have no idea,' I replied, exiting. 'I could have bonked all night, and still have bonked four more,' I sang as I left the House for the night.

That weekend I went up to Haltemprice to a hero's welcome, save for one lone voice; well, two.

Sarah, attired in her smartest lady-of-the-manor autumn finery, and I took places in the VIP pew at the Cathedral on Sunday. Sir Malachi, in full-dress uniform, with a gleaming new but empty holster dangling from his belt, sandwiched me in on the other side.

The Bishop had the temerity to finish his poxy sermon by performing some tasteless rabble-rousing.

'For Jesus said, "Turn the other cheek". I know there are some here today who sincerely believe that if Our Lord returned tomorrow He'd come armed to the teeth, and I respect their point of view. Yet God made us in His own image, though some theologians say we make God in our image, and I respect their point of view. Nonetheless, I feel constrained to vote in the House of Lords against Mr B'Stard's gun legislation, for it is written that the meek shall inherit the earth.'

As the Bishop sat down, Sir Malachi sneered into my ear, 'But they'll need armed policemen to stop the villains nicking the earth back off 'em.'

'Silly old duffer ought to be put out to grass,' I whispered.

'Isn't that why he's in the House of Lords?' Sarah giggled.

'It's not funny, Sarah. You heard him, he's voting against my Bill.' I slid down on my knees as the Bishop beckoned us to pray.

'Actually, I won't be heartbroken if your silly Bill doesn't get through. I've been thinking about it. I don't want some traffic warden with a six-shooter bearing down on me every time I double-park outside Harrods,' she blasphemed into her prayer book.

'Oh, very loyal. Amen.'

We rose to our seats. 'Sometimes I don't know why I married you,' I despaired to Heaven.

'You married me, darling, because you are *nouveau riche*

whereas my family can trace our lineage back to Edward II, and my father is Chairman of the local Conservative party and holds your seat in his gift.'

It was a rhetorical question and, anyway, Edward II had been a poof, I thought to myself as Sir Malachi's personal radio crackled out a loud but unintelligible message. He started to his feet, announcing, 'I'm on my way. There's God's work to be done outside this place!'

I fled after him, anxious to recover my property now that I'd fulfilled my part of the bargain. Catching up to Sir Malachi just as he was about to climb into his chauffeur-driven, unmarked black Jag, I panted, 'Chief Constable, what about my file?'

'Not now, B'Stard, I've just had a red alert. Suspected witchcraft in Pontefract.' The Chief Constable dismissed me with a wave of his arm.

'But you promised I could have it back once my Gun Law was passed,' I shouted as he clambered into the back seat.

Rolling down his window, Sir Malachi silenced me with a withering glance. 'It isn't passed, though, is it? Still the House of Lords to convince, and these days there are more lefties in the Lords than in the Commons. You heard the Bishop.'

I needn't have lost any slumber, not that I did. The Lords passed my Bill in spite of that jumped-up Bishop, and I now had my very own precious Gun Law. I would soon have my file back, Beatrice would look on me with new eyes (how well I know the stirring of the loins brought on by gazing on success) and I would make my bundle.

How unfair that I should be reaping the benefits of my success at just the time that my long-standing confidant and financial advisor, Norman Bormann, had fallen upon hard times, I mused as I slipped my favourite tape into the Bentley's deck.

'Now that your Gun Law has received the Royal Assent, do you expect that the presence of armed police on our streets will have a major impact on the way we life?' Robin Day asked me.

'I hope so. Otherwise, what's the point? People wouldn't be talking of me as a future Prime Minister if my Act wasn't. . . .'

'*Are* you being talked of as a future Prime?'

'Isn't that what we're doing now?'

Today Radio Four, tomorrow the world, I mused as I'd followed Norman's directions to the abandoned, overgrown marshalling yard just north of Finsbury Park.

I locked the car and trod my way carefully across muddy tracks towards the seemingly abandoned guard's carriage that was now the office of Norman Bormann.

Norman needed cheering up.

'All right, Bormann, we know you're in there. The game's up, we've got the full scam on the Chernobyl time-share scandal!' I growled as I beat on the door.

I opened the door to the smell of burning paper. Norman had taken my joke a little too seriously.

'What a ghastly place you've got here, Norman,' I said, to put him at his ease. 'Bit of a come-down for my business consultant. What happened to the plush office in Cavendish Square?'

Norman stopped feeding papers into the smouldering bin and sprayed it with a soda syphon to stop the fire. 'They finally caught up with me! The Inland Revenue, the VAT gestapo, the Fraud Squad. A chap makes fifty or sixty accounting errors. They call him a thief,' he whined.

I panicked for an instant. 'It doesn't involve me, does it?'

'No,' Norman assured me.

'Then it's not important.' I whipped Norman's handkerchief from his breast pocket and wiped off the seat of a rickety chair. 'All right, that's enough small talk. I can't afford to hang around with suspected criminals. What am I here for?'

Norman removed a gun from his jacket pocket.

'Norman, I. . . .' I ducked.

'I've found you, as you asked, a supplier of perfect copies of

Smith & Wesson .38 standard seven-shot police revolvers,' he said in triumph.

'Splendid! *Como mucho*, as we're all saying in Westminster since the visit of King Juan Carlos?' Pound signs began to spin before my eyes.

'As many as you like for ten pounds apiece,' Norman said, handing me the gun.

'It's much lighter than I thought,' I bargained, pretending to shoot Norman.

'That's because they're made out of recycled frying pans. Probably blow up if fired.'

'Oh,' I said, knocking a few thousand pounds off my mental reckonings, 'Well, not to worry. As I said in the House of Commons, they aren't for firing, they're for deterring. If you'd just give me the name and address of the supplier. . . .'

'That information will cost you,' Norman balked, which was most unlike him. He usually worked on a commission-only basis.

'How much?' I inquired, reaching into my jacket for my Gucci wallet.

'An Archer,' Norman asserted.

'A whole Jeffrey?' I gasped. 'That's two thousand pounds!' 'I need the cash, Alan,' he whined. 'And besides you'll make fifty times that selling these guns to the police.'

I couldn't dispute his maths and handed the money over to him. 'Now, where do these guns come from?'

'They're made by Mohammed Iqbal Shah International Armaments Limited,' Norman said, counting his cash.

'Oh, a Third World set-up?' I queried.

Norman fished in the bin and withdrew a charred card. 'Yes, they're in Accrington,' he said, handing me the address.

'Thanks, Norman. Bye. By the way, what's the money for, anyway? Fleeing the country?'

Norman chuckled ruefully, 'That's what they expect me to

do. No, I've decided to kill myself off.'

I made a grab for Norman's cash. 'You don't need two thousand pounds for that. Jump off something.'

'No, I'm not committing suicide,' he said, placing the money in his breast pocket, which he proceeded to caress. 'Norman Bormann is simply going to cease to exist.'

'What do you mean exactly?', I asked, curiosity getting the better of me.

'I'm going to become a woman,' Norman said, blinking at me flirtatiously from behind his Alan Whicker glasses.

I made my excuses and fled.

The moment of reckoning with Sir Malachi Jellicoe had finally arrived. Since the passing of my Act he'd become increasingly outrageous in pursuit of publicity, hitting even more national headliness, with his mystical mumbo jumbo, than I did. The mighty Chief Constable's prayers had come true through my good offices, and there he imagined he was, sitting at God's right hand, where he was convinced he would remain in the Afterlife, patrolling a heavenly police state.

I arrived at our arranged meeting place, the Hangman's Knot Inn, the same evening, shortly after opening time. The hostelry had been refurbished since my return to Parliament, no doubt with all the money I'd handed over the bar to our genial host Sidney Bliss during my campaign. Ah, yes, my lips still automatically puckered recalling the many happy hours spent pouring drinks down the natives' throats and kissing anything that was capable of voting; disused mineworkers, gurning old ladies, burly rugger types, not to mention a few buxom wenches and Beatrice Protheroe, when I could lay my hands on her.

I admired the new décor as I strode into the Public, Sidney had replaced the old horse brasses and toby jugs with a giant-sized oil painting of Chief Executioner Pierrepoint, his boss until hanging had been suspended, surrounded by black-and-white framed photographs of nondescript-looking gentlemen with low foreheads and crazy eyes, 'clients', presumably. Draped round the shelves of the bar were swathes of rope nooses interspersed with black hoods, lending a sober if somewhat nautical air to the place.

Several of the natives were occupying their brains with mindless games like dominoes and chequers. They all touched their caps in respect for me as I made my way to the bar. I nodded and waved and assured them all that I could continue to have their interests at heart.

Sidney greeted me from behind the bar with more enthusiasm than normal. 'Good evening, sir! Great day for you, sir! You've struck a blow for Law and Order, sir!' He crunched my hand in his and pumped it up and down in painful enthusiasm.

'Yes, I have had a pretty good day,' I replied modestly, clenching and unclenching my right hand to get the circulation going again. 'And how about you, Sidney?'

'Me, sir? I haven't had a good day since they abolished hanging. You did promise you'd bring back the rope,' he pleaded, hope lighting up his lugubrious features.

'I'm trying, Sidney,' I sighed. 'But it's a long haul to the short drop. . . .'

'I haven't lost the knack, sir,' Sidney enthused. He took a tankard from its hook and pulled a pint of Samuel Smith's with one powerful jerk of the pump handle to prove his point. He pushed the tankard toward me with, 'Here you are, sir. On the house.'

'Thank you, Sidney,' I demurred. 'But I'd prefer a large brandy . . . on the house. After all, the police won't dare breathalyse me tonight.'

'Where's Sir Malachi, in the Snug?' I asked as he handed me a double brandy. Sidney nodded. 'What's he drinking?'

'Dandelion and burdock and a pint of bitter for his friend,' Sidney said, reaching under the bar for another bottle. I shook my head. That bastard had already had enough freebies from me to last his lifetime.

'Friend? He's supposed to be alone,' I muttered in confusion, entering the Snug, where the Chief Constable was indeed alone doing the pools, with his half-finished drink beside him. A full pint of bitter and an unopened packet of pork scratchings were neatly arranged on the table in front of the chair opposite him.

'This one's sure as eggs is eggs. Really? Charlton to win at Liverpool? No, no, if you say so,' the nutter was murmuring to himself as I approached.

I cleared my throat noisily to draw his attention. 'Good evening, Chief Constable.'

Sir Malachi looked up, startled, then raised his glass to me. 'Here's to you, B'Stard. You've struck a blow for Justice and Jesus today.'

I started to sit in the chair opposite, but Sir Malachi tugged me to my feet, exclaiming, 'Don't sit there, that's someone's seat.'

I sat down next to him, saying 'Have you brought it with you?' The less time I spent socialising with this loony the better.

'Brought what?' the Chief Constable glared at me in confusion.

'My dossier!' I hissed. The old fart was really out to lunch.

'Oh, that,' Sir Malachi waved one hand at me in a dismissive gesture and with the other pulled an enormous pearl-handled revolver from his holster, saying, 'What do you think of this?'

'Very nice,' I humoured him.

'I wasn't talking to you,' Sir Malachi barked. 'Yes, it's a .45 Colt Frontiersman. Blow the balls off one of those flying pickets at fifty yards! Yes, they really would be airborne.' The Chief Constable spun the bullet chamber and levelled his sights at my forehead.

'Very nice. Now let's put it back in its little house,' I crooned to him as I would a small child, and guided his gun hand back to his holster.

'You promised I could have my dossier back,' I asserted, much relieved.

'Oh, you mean the dossier that proves you were responsible for that tragic car crash on the eve of the General Election,' Sir Malachi bellowed.

'Shh!' I cautioned.

Sir Malachi leaned across the table and said in a conspiratorial tone, 'It's all right, He knows.' He cocked his ear and, nodding twice, continued, 'The Almighty reckons it would be silly to give us this useful hold over you when there's so much more of his work to be done.'

I finally twigged. Addressing the empty chair, I posited, 'Almighty, suppose I built you a church?'

'The Lord of Hosts doesn't need any more churches,' the Chief Constable interjected into my private conversation with the Lord. 'He needs you to work for him in Parliament. For example, how about a Bill to criminalise atheism?'

'Yes! Good idea! Great idea!' I was learning how to play this particular three-hander fast. 'But you've both got to realise, the chances against a backbencher getting a Bill through are a thousand to one. I was incredibly lucky to do so well in the ballot for Private Members' Bills this time.'

'He thinks it was luck!' Sir Malachi chuckled to his invisible Friend.

'I see, you mean a miracle? Who am I to cavil or demur?' I raised my glass to toast the Host.

'That's the spirit that moves mountains!' Sir Malachi voiced his approval while tearing open the packet of pork scratchings with his teeth. 'Have a pork scratching, saith the Lord.'

I took a couple for the sake of politeness, thanking him and Him. 'There's just one problem. Even with heavenly help, Bills take time to get through, and we'll be giving the forces of darkness time to build up their power. . . .'

'You mean Lucifer?' The Chief Constable clapped his hands over his mouth.

'I mean the Bishop of Haltemprice,' I intoned darkly.

Sir Malachi laughed, 'That old fool? He doesn't bother us!'

'He should. Don't you remember his sermon? "I respect atheists, idolators and cannibals," he said. He opposed the Gun Act, and we all know that was God's will . . . and he's against your censorship campaign. And last Christmas, when you were away on pilgrimage duty, he preached that not only was Mary not a virgin, she was technically a surrogate mother!'

My oratory did not fall on deaf ears.

'He never did!' The Chief Constable choked on his pork scratchings in his astonishment.

'Cross my heart,' I swore, making the appropriate liturgical motions. 'In fact, not only is the Bishop almost certainly an unbeliever; I suspect he is the secret leader of all who oppose the will of God!'

'You don't mean . . .?' Sir Malachi leaned close to me and gabbled. 'That's right, the Antichrist!' I exclaimed in a hushed but awesome tone.

Sir Malachi struck his forehead with his hand. 'Yes, of course. It all adds up.' He leaned across the table, asking, 'What do you think?'

After a short pause, Sir Malachi announced, 'The Almighty says you're right! Here,' he said reaching beneath his seat and withdrawing my file, 'your dossier. He says it's the least we can do. I'm on my way.'

Sir Malachi sped from the room like a dervish. I opened up my briefcase, kissed the folder, and got out my personal cell phone.

I ate the remaining pork scratchings while waiting to be connected to Deputy Chief Ginsburg, who, sure as shooting, would want to know something to his advantage. I looked forward to doing business with him.

An hour later I arrived home, poured myself a large scotch and relaxed with my file. I glanced through it until I'd formulated a plan that would work.

Norman had really let the Luigi episode get out of control, which was unlike him. The file even included a cheque signed by him on behalf of All's Fare (Travel) Ltd, made out to Luigi Corleone for the five thousand pounds I'd given Norman in cash before the 'accident' and marked 'return to drawer', a company report on All's Fare listing Norman and myself as sole company directors of that lucrative little sideline and, most incriminating of all, a letter from Luigi himself to Sir Malachi, which totally blew our gaff. The letter said:

11 June 1987
2 Strada Vecchio
Napoli

Dear Sir Chief Constable,
I am writing to you from where you cannot catch me now since only you can see that justice must be done. I demand Omerta! It is my right.

I am a simple ice-cream vendor and until June of this year anno domini 1987 was happy selling my coronets threw out the streets of Haltemprice Village. 25p for a single scoop and 55p for a double with flaky choc. It was not much, but it was a descent honest living until one day some bloke in a suit and glasses like that man on telly wears came up to me and ordered a single scoop of strawberry and put to me an offer I could not refuse. For the loudspeaker from my van that plays my jolly jingles and two hours of my time Saturday aft. £5,000 – enough to get my wife and myself and our seven bambinos to Napoli where I was born on holiday to see my sainted Mama one last time before she passes as she is eighty-seven and well nackered.

I paid for the tickets on my credit card – no problem then only now. My credit limit is £10,000.

I turned up at the stables like I was told in my van and wearing my usual white uniform that my wife stays up all night washing and ironing. You have to look clean in my line of work or the punters will guess. This man in the glasses and the suit who told me to call him Mr Bee gave me a badge to wear saying Tonys Tannoys like the sign said on the stable door only that also said special rates – election bonanza sale or something. There was all ready one rusty old tannoy in the yard and Mr Bee made me remove mine from the van and then park it in the shit behind the stables out of sight like.

We are expecting two customers Mr Bee told me. I want you to in stall the tannoys and take a good long time fiddling about. He also told me to saw a little into the brake cable of one car and to do something to the steering of the other one. Lucky my van breaks down often and I tinker with motors all the time I told him. He left and promised to be back at 4 p.m. with the cash.

Sure enough a Volvo and a Cortina came in and I done the necessary. The bloke in the Cortina tipped me £2.

Mr Bee came back at 4 and gave me this cheque for £5,000. He said he couldn't get the cash after all seeing it was Saturday and the banks are shut. The cheque bounced as you can see. All I got for my days work was £2. Is that fair?

I request you find this crook and make him pay. Jesus Christ is on my side. I am stuck in Napoli until the money comes threw as I have now gone over my credit limit. We can come to some deal when I get back.

Yours faithfully
Luigi Tomaso Corleone

I destroyed the letter and the cheque and tried to ring Norman. I was angry enough to cut his balls off before his surgeon took my opportunity away, but the operator told me his line had been disconnected.

I was just wondering whether to employ a hitman to hit the

previous hitman when I heard Sarah's key in the door. She was back from Evensong.

'Daddy's not going to like this one little bit,' Sarah warned over breakfast on Sunday morning. 'He said you're completely ignoring the constituency's interest in the furtherment of your own career. You haven't even had one surgery since the election, and old Barker-Thisby, however senile he was in the end, used to have surgeries regularly every Friday evening and Saturday morning for the past twenty-five years, and they were well attended. It's what the people here want; it's what the people here need. And Beatrice thinks so as well. What with your gallivanting off to New York or Los Angeles or Timbuctoo for all I know every few weeks, the people here have even forgotten what you look like.'

'I don't know how that can be,' I retorted. 'My picture's in the papers at least twice a week. And there was that big piece in the *Tatler* last month. Though, on second thoughts I hope they didn't see that one. "Alan B'Stard, self-styled Leader of the Prat Pack", indeed!' I slurped my cornflakes in noisy indignation.

'Don't worry, darling,' Sarah sneered, crashing her tea cup down on its saucer. 'I'm sure the mineworkers and sheep farmers just haven't had time to open their copies of the *Tatler* yet. Honestly, Alan, the very least you could do is attend a service in the Cathedral each Sunday to remind them you're their MP,' she whinged on. Sarah is particularly unattractive in full-complaint. Her nose flares and twitches like a cross between a thoroughbred horse and a demented rabbit. Give me Beatrice any day, who never loses her cool.

'I've got bigger fish to fry this morning,' I said. 'But I promise I'll go next week, Fluffy Tail.'

'Well, I'm off to Matins,' Sarah threw over her shoulder as she flounced out of the dining room, obviously unplacated. I sat there thinking about Beatrice, who doubtless fancied me as much as I fancied her. Pity she wouldn't mix business with pleasure. I recalled yesterday at dinner at Sir Roland's when I'd squeezed Beatrice's thigh under the table and encountered Sarah's hand entwined in hers on her lap. Ah well, at least it was nice to see old school friends still so close. With a sigh I got up. It was time to meet Ginsburg.

At lunchtime, Sarah reported to me what had taken place in the Cathedral that morning, revelling in the drama of it. Seemingly our little tiff was over.

'We were in the middle of singing "Oh Lamb of God", my favourite, so poignant don't you agree, darling, when Sir Malachi Jellicoe crashed through the Cathedral doors and stormed down the aisle toward the Bishop bellowing, "Get ye behind me, Bishop. The game's up!" You know how good the Cathedral's acoustics are, don't you? Well, it was truly thunderous. Remember that film *Moses*? He sounded just like that. Vintage Hollywood stuff.'

'Good gracious. How frightful, darling!' I exclaimed. 'What happened then?' As if I didn't already know. I'd been only twenty yards away at the time.

'Well, Sir Malachi got to about ten feet in front of the Bishop and shouted, "Come on, Beelzebub, make my day!" or some other fool thing, and pulled two enormous pearl-handled revolvers from his hip holsters, just like John Wayne, only evil. The Bishop froze. He just stood there and was only saved by the choir from being shot to bits by that maniac. Only they weren't the real choir, they were a Special Patrol Group who'd been tipped off somehow, thank God. They drew their guns, which they'd had hidden under their cassocks, and jumped Sir Malachi, who let off a couple of shots into the air before he was completely overpowered by them. By some miracle, no one was hurt and Sir Malachi was led off kicking and screaming, to the bin, I hope, but they're sure to cover it up,' Sarah finished, her eyes gleaming.

'Sorry I missed it,' I said plaintively. 'Too bad church isn't always that exciting.'

'Yes, it was rather exciting,' she laughed.

'Seriously, dearest, didn't it teach you something?' I rocked back in my chair in my most portentous parliamentary pose. 'Didn't it prove to you that the Bishop and a lot of other innocent, God-fearing folk might have been slaughtered by that demented old fool if it hadn't been for my Gun Law?'

'You could say that,' she pondered.

'I just did, Fluffy Tail.'

While Sarah had been in the Cathedral witnessing what was by her account a first-rate show, I myself was sitting with Deputy Chief Constable Ginsburg in an unmarked special operations van in the Cathedral yard, listening to the performance on his personal radio.

'That's it!' Ginsburg clicked the radio off triumphantly. 'It's all over, they've got the straitjacket on the *meshugana*.'

I peered out of the reinforced smoke-glass window. Sir Malachi was being hauled out of the Cathedral in a straitjacket by four ruddy-faced policemen in full choral drag.

Ginsburg crossed to the window and clucked his tongue at the sorry scene.

'He never should have passed his probationary period. He was hearing voices ten years before the introduction of personal radios. You've done the Force a good turn, Sir, grassing on that sky jockey!

'Just doing my public duty, Deputy Constable Ginsburg . . . sorry,' I corrected myself as we shook hands. 'Chief Constable Ginsburg.'

'That's right, now I'm the *gunsa macha*!' Chief Constable Ginsburg chortled. 'So, if there's any little favour I can do you . . .?'

'Well . . . Has your Force placed a bulk order for handguns yet?'

As Ginsburg shook his head, I added pointedly, 'Because I can get them for you wholesale. . . .'

All in all, a very profitable week-end's work, I summed up to myself as I sped along the motorway past the Watford Gap back to London. The Bentley was doing one hundred and ten and the engine wasn't even feeling the strain. Great British workmanship! I vowed to write to the Chairman tomorrow to see if I could do anything to further his export drive. A promotional jaunt to Dallas or Denver, maybe?

I was mentally composing the letter as my cell phone rang. It was Norman with the great news that the Hertfordshire Police had purchased five hundred guns yesterday.

As I pushed the button to turn off the phone's speaker, I spied a local police car, its blue light flashing furiously, closing up behind me. Before I even had a chance to brake, a gun appeared out of the police car window aimed at my back tyre. How dare he have the temerity? I'd done the police more good than Robert Peel, I thought with fury as, with an enormous bang and a flash of light, the police car veered off on to the soft shoulder.

I shrugged and played 'Money for Nothing and the Chicks for free', my second favourite tape, all the way home.

CHAPTER TWO

PASSPORT TO FREEDOM

It was a dusky early October afternoon a fortnight later. The leaves were falling and my temporary secretary Victoria had already fallen. For the smooth, sexy man-about-town in the driving seat next to her, that is.

We sped in the gathering gloom to the Heathrow Grange Hotel for a little 'dictation' before my flight the next morning to Dusseldorf. Not quite Dallas or Denver, but the Chairman of Rolls Royce was still considering my proposal, his PA had told me. I caressed the handbrake of my faithful six-litre steed. Victoria caressed my knee and sighed, 'Sexy.' Our eyes met in the rearview mirror and I mouthed a kiss at her. She wriggled, pearls all ajingle, as we crunched to a stop in the gravel of the hotel carpark.

Victoria was already flushed and trembling with anticipation as we entered the room. I shut the door and she dropped my attaché case and moaned. God, she was going to be a hot one.

I pulled her toward me. We kissed, unzipped and unbuttoned each other, fumbling in our eagerness to unite. We flopped on to the bed and writhed a bit, her soft naked skin silken against my hard muscled frame. Okay, Victoria, one hump or two, I thought, readying myself to oblige her.

Suddenly the little cow went rigid. She rolled off me and switched on the bedside light.

'Okay, we'll do it with the light on,' I shrugged and resumed my fondling.

'I'm sorry, I don't know if I can go through with this,' she said, pulling away from me and staring into space, lips pursed. 'Well, do you mind if I start without you?' I rubbed myself against her to arouse her again.

'I mean, I just don't do one night stands,' she hedged.

'I wish you'd told me earlier. This is the Heathrow Grange Hotel. These rooms don't come cheap. I haven't come here to sleep,' I complained indignantly.

Victoria bounded from the bed and retrieved her bra from the floor. Putting her arms through its shoulder straps, she started weeping. 'That's a horrible thing to say!'

Was it? I thought. I leaped up to placate her. 'Is it? I'm only joking,' I said swiftly. 'I'm renowned in Westminster for my sense of humour, my enormous majority . . . and my incredible virility. And Vicky,' I continued, removing her bra again, 'This isn't a one-nighter, it's a first-nighter. I love you. I've loved you ever since Sloaney Girl Temp Agency sent you into my life yesterday.'

'Do you really mean that?' she asked, with tear-sparkled eyes.

'Of course I do,' I soothed her, pulling her back on to the bed. Victoria turned off the bedside lamp and we quickly consummated my passion.

I rolled out from under her and turned the lamp on again, asking politely, 'How was it for you?'

'How was what?' Victoria asked, still dazed in the aftermath of spent passion, I guess. 'Oh! Well it was . . . different.'

I folded my hands behind my head on the pillow and asked with pride, 'In what way different? Sexier? Chunkier? Raunchier?'

Victoria paused for a moment, trying to find the right adjective in her somewhat limited vocabulary. 'Quicker,' she finally said.

'Of course it was quick, I'm a busy man. I haven't got time to waste,' I hissed. Stupid girl. 'Anyway, I've never understood this obsession with quantity over quality. Orgasm's the objective, isn't it?' I pointed out to her, adding, 'The magazines my wifes reads are full of articles about how to have orgasms, though why they're printing them in *Farmer's Weekly* is beyond me. Well, I've never had any trouble on the climax front. Whoops, just had another one,' I joked, unwinding the twisted sheets from my legs. 'I wonder what's on TV,' I said, and leaped out of bed to turn the set on.

'Alan,' Victoria called to me plaintively. 'Did you mean it when you said you loved me?'

'Of course when I said I loved you, I meant it,' I reassured her, climbing back into bed.

'Only I've never been to bed with a married man before . . . not unless you count Daddy,' Victoria prattled on.

'Shh . . . this is my favourite commercial,' I silenced her and sand 'Say the Leeds and you're smiling . . .' along with the television.

'I'm so awfully glad you love me, because I'm not on the Pill,' Victoria announced. I stopped singing and pricked up my ears.

'I was on the Pill, but I put on two stone and got spots and no one fancied me. What would you do if I got pregnant, Alan?'

'Leave my wife and marry you, of course,' I promised, the conventional Tory line in these matters. 'In fact, I'll phone my wife now.'

'Alan, darling, you'r so impetuous!' Victoria exclaimed, pawing me as I dialed the code.

'Oh be quiet, you stupid typist,' I shrugged her off and dialed the remainder of the number. I had promised to phone Sarah from Germany tonight. Really no need to practise such a deception, but I didn't want my technique to go rusty.

'Hello, is dot Haltemprice fumf, fumf, drei, swei? I haf a Herr B'Stard callink vrom Dusseldorf,' I said in my finest German accent as Sarah answered the phone. 'Hello, darling,' I continued in my normal voice, 'This is me calling from Germany.'

'Hello, Thumper,' Sarah responded in a mellow voice. 'How was the flight?'

'Fine. Terribly efficient. You know what the Germans are like,' I prevaricated as Victoria covered my shoulders with little soundless kisses.

'Not really, but daddy does. He killed heaps in the war,' Sarah replied.

'Anyway, I just called to say I love you,' I said. Sarah confirmed that she loved me too. 'And you are the rudest, sexiest rabbit I have ever come across,' I added, and bussed Sarah a big one into the mouthpiece. Victoria began to wail. I quickly silenced her with a pillow as Sarah said her good-byes. 'Goodbye or *auf weidersehen*.' I concluded breezily and hung up.

Victoria was already halfway out the door when I turned round. I turned off the light and quickly fell asleep, exhausted by our rigorous sexual antics.

I'd forgotten to ask the Reception Desk for an alarm call, and by the time I'd made myself a cup of coffee with the equipment thoughtfully provided by the management, showered, dressed and stowed everything in my expandable executive attaché case, I was running very late.

There was a long queue for my Dusseldorf flight, but Piers and Bob Crippen were very near the front. I hurried up to them and dropped my suitcase in front of Piers, saying suavely, 'Thanks for keeping my place, Piers. Overslept; you know what it's like when you're in the saddle all night boffing some insatiable little sexpot. No, you don't know what it's like at all,' I added in response to Pier's look of bemusement.

Comrade Crippen poked me in the shoulder, shouting angrily, 'Hey, pal, there's a queue here, you know.' Talk about stating the obvious.

'Don't fret, Crippen,' I soothed him, 'It's an airliner, not a corporation tram. There are seats for everyone!' His scowling face goaded me into continuing, 'Though heaven knows why

'Hello, Thumper,' Sarah responded in a mellow voice. 'How was the flight?'

'Fine. Terribly efficient. You know what the Germans are like,' I prevaricated as Victoria covered my shoulders with little soundless kisses.

'Not really, but daddy does. He killed heaps in the war,' Sarah replied.

'Anyway, I just called to say I love you,' I said. Sarah confirmed that she loved me too. 'And you are the rudest, sexiest rabbit I have ever come across,' I added, and bussed Sarah a big one into the mouthpiece. Victoria began to wail. I quickly silenced her with a pillow as Sarah said her good-byes. 'Goodbye or *auf weidersehen*.' I concluded breezily and hung up.

Victoria was already halfway out the door when I turned round. I turned off the light and quickly fell asleep, exhausted by our rigorous sexual antics.

I'd forgotten to ask the Reception Desk for an alarm call, and by the time I'd made myself a cup of coffee with the equipment thoughtfully provided by the management, showered, dressed and stowed everything in my expandable executive attaché case, I was running very late.

There was a long queue for my Dusseldorf flight, but Piers and Bob Crippen were very near the front. I hurried up to them and dropped my suitcase in front of Piers, saying suavely, 'Thanks for keeping my place, Piers. Overslept; you know what it's like when you're in the saddle all night boffing some insatiable little sexpot. No, you don't know what it's like at all,' I added in response to Pier's look of bemusement.

Comrade Crippen poked me in the shoulder, shouting angrily, 'Hey, pal, there's a queue here, you know.' Talk about stating the obvious.

'Don't fret, Crippen,' I soothed him, 'It's an airliner, not a corporation tram. There are seats for everyone!' His scowling face goaded me into continuing, 'Though heaven knows why this obsession with quantity over quality. Orgasm's the objective, isn't it?' I pointed out to her, adding, 'The magazines my wifes reads are full of articles about how to have orgasms, though why they're printing them in *Farmer's Weekly* is beyond me. Well, I've never had any trouble on the climax front. Whoops, just had another one,' I joked, unwinding the twisted sheets from my legs. 'I wonder what's on TV,' I said, and leaped out of bed to turn the set on.

'Alan,' Victoria called to me plaintively. 'Did you mean it when you said you loved me?'

'Of course when I said I loved you, I meant it,' I reassured her, climbing back into bed.

'Only I've never been to bed with a married man before . . . not unless you count Daddy,' Victoria prattled on.

'Shh . . . this is my favourite commercial,' I silenced her and sand 'Say the Leeds and you're smiling . . .' along with the television.

'I'm so awfully glad you love me, because I'm not on the Pill,' Victoria announced. I stopped singing and pricked up my ears.

'I was on the Pill, but I put on two stone and got spots and no one fancied me. What would you do if I got pregnant, Alan?'

'Leave my wife and marry you, of course,' I promised, the conventional Tory line in these matters. 'In fact, I'll phone my wife now.'

'Alan, darling, you'r so impetuous!' Victoria exclaimed, pawing me as I dialed the code.

'Oh be quiet, you stupid typist,' I shrugged her off and dialed the remainder of the number. I had promised to phone Sarah from Germany tonight. Really no need to practise such a deception, but I didn't want my technique to go rusty.

'Hello, is dot Haltemprice fumf, fumf, drei, swei? I haf a Herr B'Stard callink vrom Dusseldorf,' I said in my finest German accent as Sarah answered the phone. 'Hello, darling,' I continued in my normal voice, 'This is me calling from Germany.'

you're going to a farming conference when you represent an inner city slum.'

'Even my constituents are allowed to eat,' The Red said.

'Are they? Pity,' I riposted.

That really annoyed Crippen as much as it was supposed to. 'If this terminal wasn't patrolled by heavily armed members of the Anti-Terrorist Squad, I'd give you a good smack for that!'

'See?' I addressed the queue in general. 'There is the voice of the modern Labour party. Thinly veiled political thuggery.' Crippen sidled up to me. 'Do you like hospital food?' he threatened.

'Love it,' I assured him. 'But then of course I'm in BUPA.'

For a second I thought I'd gone too far and that he was going to give me a Liverpool kiss. Fortunately, three of his comrades dragged me away before he could break my nose with his bullet head. How uncouth. He checked in and I then proceeded to hand my own ticket to the Valkyrie in uniform behind the check-in desk.

'Your passport, please, Herr B'Stard,' she ordered.

I put my suitcase on the weighing machine and she hurled it on to the moving conveyor belt behind her after tagging it. I searched through my pockets for my passport. It wasn't anywhere to be found. 'I'm sure I had it last night,' I muttered to myself, which made Piers snigger.

'There's a long line behind you. Would you please stand aside?' the Rhine maiden barked.

'As Hitler said to Chamberlain before he invaded Poland,' I couldn't help quipping as I double-checked my pockets. I blushed, suffering the instant recollection of my passport back on my bedside table in Haltemprice.

Snorting, she chucked my ticket on to the adjacent counter. 'Next please,' she dismissed me.

'Listen, my dear,' I said patiently, standing my ground. 'I am Alan B'Stard MP. I have the biggest majority in the House of Commons and I am attending a conference on a subject close to the German soul, namely pigmeat. I don't need a passport; we won the war.' Look, Fraulein, I can vouch for him,' Piers chipped in loyally.

'Yes,' she hissed. 'But who will vouch for you?'

We looked around for Crippen and our other colleagues, but they'd already gone through Passport Control. 'Oh,' Piers said lamely. 'Alan will vouch for me.'

I thumped on the desk. 'I demand to see the manager, or the airportführer, or whatever you call him.' I knew my rights. 'I'm afraid Mr Goering is unavailable. He's busy pillaging the art galleries of Eastern Europe,' she joked Germanically with that annoying air of authority people muster when wearing any kind of uniform.

'Smoking or non-smoking?' She dismissed me and addressed Piers. He handed over his ticket and passport as he ruminated, 'Perhaps it's in your attaché case.'

'What?' I asked impatiently, still fuming.

'Your passport,' he prompted, taking his boarding pass and moving out of the queue.

'No,' I grunted. 'I must have left it in Yorkshire. Damn!'

Piers bent down and lifted my attaché case from the floor. He proffered it to me, pleading. 'At least look in your case. . . .'

'It's not in my case,' I said emphatically.

'It might be. I'm always losing things and then finding them in unexpected places,' he continued doggedly.

'That's because you are a congenital idiot!' I told him.

Piers snatched the case from my hands and snapped open the latches before I could stop him. Three hotel towels, a bathmat, an ashtray and the electric kettle thumped and clattered loudly round our feet. I could feel everyone in the airport staring at me.

'God,' I addressed the tittering queue, shaking my head sadly. 'The lengths these hotels will go to to attract VIP customers.' I made Piers pick up and pack my belongings before he departed.

My nimble brain had never let me down before, so why should it now? I encouraged myself as I drove the Bentley into East Yorkshire. I'd always been able to slip into anything I wanted and slide out of boring, awkward situations before, and this time would be no different. I rehearsed my chosen explanation.

'I don't know if I told you that we all had to have routine blood tests a few weeks ago and they phoned the results through to us this morning. Naturally, once they found out Piers's AIDS test was positive, they flew us all home immediately.' Yes, that was it. It was simple, like Piers.

Sarah was on the sofa in the drawing room, surrounded with what looked like brochures featuring property in the West Indies. I had thought we were going to spend Christmas at home. Oh well, we both could do with a little sunshine. She looked up at me and smiled quizzically as I entered the room.

'I know what you're going to say! What on earth am I doing back in England in the middle of the conference?' I pre-empted her breezily. 'Well, you're not going to believe this, but we all had routine blood tests last month and Piers, of all people, turns out to be. . . .' Sarah interrupted my flow by flourishing my passport. 'You left it in your bedside drawer,' she smirked.

'I know. Under the March 1987 Amendment to the European Community Travel Agreement, Members of Parliament on official businesses do not need. . . .' I started.

'Oh, shut up, Alan,' she sneered. 'I'm not Piers! Why don't you just admit you spent last night in an airport hotel with some little typist, for whom I feel nothing but the deepest pity?'

'I see,' I observed, rocking back on my heels. 'Well if you prefer to think the worst rather than listen to my perfectly reasonable explanation, quite honestly, darling, I don't know how this marriage is going to survive.'

'It isn't,' Sarah announced casually. 'I've just inherited a million pounds and I'm going to divorce you.'

I blinked rapidly a number of times. This must be a bad dream; she couldn't be serious. But she was. In a triumphal voice she exclaimed that an uncle she hadn't even known was still alive had died and left her two hundred thousand shares in Ocelot Motors and that she no longer had any reason to stick my behaviour. She and her lover, whoever he was, were going far away. The divorce would be messy, she assured me as she went into the kitchen.

I stood speechless, then dropped heavily onto the vacated sofa, which was still warm from Sarah's rump. I put my head in my hands in despair. How could she desert me in my hour of need? I thought of the publicity; I thought of Sir Roland. Oh God, I could easily lose my seat.

Sarah returned with a chilled bottle of champagne and two glasses. Effortlessly she popped the cork. She handed one to me, which I downed in one gulp.

'Up yours,' she toasted me, with a glittering smile.

Naturally I got on the blower to Norman as soon as I could and, leaving the Bentley in the House carpark, I arrived at Norman's new hideaway at noon by taxi as he requested. It was a decrepit, rusting ancient dormobile parked on double-yellow lines just outside the Grosvenor House Hotel.

'Edwina Currie likes it hot and spicy,' I hollered through the door.

'Does she?' Norman shouted from inside the dormobile.

'That's the password, isn't it?' I confirmed.

'Oh,' said Norman vaguely as he opened the door, his two-day growth of grizzled beard glinting in the sunlight.

I clambered in, observing, 'You know you've been wheel-clamped?'

Norman smiled in a patronising manner. 'Of course. That's the whole object of the exercise.'

'What do you mean?' I asked, perplexed. Was he losing his marbles as well as his balls?

Norman gestured round his cramped quarters, declaring, 'It's a matter of perception. You see a clapped-out dormobile, immobilised by vindictive traffic wardens. I see a hundred square feet of prime office space in Park Lane, fifty pounds a day and no rates.'

I looked at him with renewed respect. 'Are you wearing make-up?'

'Just a hint of mascara,' Norman admitted, and batted his lashes at me.

'It suits you,' I offered.

Norman cleared his throat in embarrassment and said in a businesslike tone, 'As soon as you told me about the divorce, I transferred all your companies to the one country where even the bank accounts of known criminals are safe from official scrutiny.'

I thought quickly. 'You mean the Vatican?'

Norman nodded. 'Precisely. So your wife won't be able to get her hands on a penny.'

'That's very good, Norman,' I approved. 'But the problem isn't my money. Sarah's inherited a major stake in Ocelot Motors. That's why she can afford to divorce me!'

'I see.' Norman reassessed the situation. 'If she's not after your money, it doesn't matter if she leaves you, does it? And if I were your wife. . . .' He hesitated, confused, and looked at me for further explanation.

'Listen, I'm only MP for Haltemprice because Sarah's father runs the local Conservative party. The second we're divorced I'll be out on my arse with about as much chance of finding another seat as a deaf kid in a game of musical chairs.' I put it in a succinct nutshell for him.

Norman beckoned me to sit down on one of the bunks. He went to sit behind his desk. 'Oh, it's serious then. I suppose you want me to come up with some ingenious solution?'

I interrupted his meaningful pause with, 'I suppose you want me to continue to pay for your sex change treatment. . . .'

Norman contemplated the greasy vinyl ceiling thoughtfully. 'Has she actually got the shares in her possession yet?' he asked eventually.

'No, I don't think so. Her uncle died abroad, so there are all the legal formalities to go through first,' I replied.

'Good,' Norman said emphatically. 'That gives you a little time. . . .'

'To do what?' I frowned, not catching his drift.

'It's obvious,' Norman smiled. 'Destroy the company.'

'Thereby turning Sarah's shares into waste paper. That's brilliant, Norman.' I paused to reflect. 'No, it's not. We're not talking about Joe's Garage! Ocelot is a major sports car producer!'

'So was De Lorean, and they went bust,' Norman countered.

'Ocelot aren't De Lorean. Ocelot make proper cars that work,' I despaired.

'So stop them,' Norman challenged me.

I may have been accused of many things in my life, but never of failing to grasp the nettle. In the taxi back to the House I mulled over the prickly problem of bankrupting Ocelot Motors before Sarah could ruin me, and by late that afternoon I'd set the wheels, well, Piers, in motion. Piers is a barrister and though he is emphatically not a secret member of Mensa, in fact had never practised, I felt certain that his legal training and his tendency to worry a problem until it was bored to death would come in handy, at least in a menial research capacity.

Waiting for Piers to come up trumps, I poured myself a brandy and flicked through the pile of *Financial Timeses* Sir Stephen keeps beside his desk to fool everyone he has his finger on the financial pulse of the nation, looking for any mention of

Ocelot. There were quite a number, unfortunately all favourable; CBI Special Awards left right and centre, Institute of Directors' accolades. So far, so depressing.

The office phone rang. I answered it with alacrity, hoping it was Piers with good tidings. It was Victoria, the temp I'd tupped, with the wonderful news that I was probably going to follow in the footsteps of Cecil Parkinson. Just what I needed. I curbed my temper and played it cool.

'Have a very hot bath and drink a bottle of gin, and if that doesn't work, call me tomorrow,' I snapped!

Piers entered the room, carrying sheaves of paper. I curtailed Victoria's whines, 'No, of course I don't love you. Grow up, Victoria.'

Slamming down the receiver, I looked expectantly at Piers and exclaimed, 'Where have you been? I sent you to the library hours ago. I hope you haven't been wasting your time voting.'

'The photocopying machine broke down. I had to wait for the man . . .'

'Then you should have copied them out by hand,' I exploded. 'Come on, give me. . . .'

Childishly, Piers hid my papers behind his back and pouted, 'I'm not your servant, Alan.'

'If you were I'd have sacked you long ago,' I retorted, and took a sip of brandy.

'Er,' he wheedled, 'do you think I could have a drink?'

Piers put the papers on my desk and I grabbed them eagerly. 'I don't see why not. Just make sure you're back from the bar by eleven. I might need you.' I dismissed him with a wave. He sat disconsolately and opened a magazine.

'Right, "Company Report 1986–87. Profits up thirty-four per cent; dividends up forty-two percent; exports up sixty-one per cent; workforce up by 3,500. . . ." '

'Makes you proud to be British, doesn't it?' Said Piers with an owlish grin.

'Shut up, Piers!' I expostulated and continued reading the report aloud. ' "No-strike agreement for further five years. . . ." It would be easier to bankrupt Jeffrey Archer!' I said, hurling the report on to the desk.

'Listen to this!' Piers exclaimed, startling me from my gloomy reverie. ' "The latest Ocelot 3.8 Turbo Supercat, built at their new £200 million factory in Bramall, is a world beater. My test model sleekly-muscled its way from nought to sixty in seven and a half seconds. . . ." Wish I had one,' he added plaintively.

'What are you droning on about?' I moaned.

He showed me the front of the magazine, 'It's not me, it's Anneka Rice, writing in this month's' issue of *Yuppie Car*. I wish I was a Yuppie.' Then, a moment later, Piers dropped the magazine back on to his lap and asked me, 'What does "yuppie" actually mean?'

'Yuppie is short for "Useless Pill", so you are one. Congratulations,' I replied in exasperation, toasting him with my empty brandy glass. 'Don't be spiteful' Piers whined.

I got up to pour myself a fresh brandy, a brainwave just teasing the back of my mind, waiting to erupt. I asked idly, 'Piers, where did you say Ocelot had their new factory?'

'I'm not telling you,' Piers taunted me, piqued. So I pinched his arm hard, Piers cried, 'Brammall, Brammall, a place called Brammal. . . .!!'

'Bramall?' Eureka! I had found it. 'That's Crippen's constituency! Piers, you're a genius!' I congratulated him. 'Come on, we're going to break into the Prime Minister's office!' 'Right' said Piers.

I put my arm round him and led him to the door. Then my words sank in, Piers shrank back and said gravely, 'Oh no. I draw the line there, Alan. I know I let you talk me into all sorts of things because I'm frightened of you, but I'm more frightened of Her!'

I gave his shoulder a heartening squeeze. 'If you help me, I'll get you one of those Ocelot Supercats,' I whispered seductively as I led him into the corridor.

'Do you promise?' Piers asked, wide-eyed.

'No' I told him. 'But I promise that if you don't help me. I won't get you a supercat.'

Piers was still trying to work this out as I hauled him downstairs to the Principal Floor. As we approached the corridor leading to the Prime Minister's Office I adopted my nonchalant air, which was the only way to carry this off. Piers, of course, was spoiling my act, looking as furtive as the proverbial cat who crept into the crypt.

'Piers,' I admonished him in a whisper from the side of my mouth. 'Will you stop tiptoeing along like Wee Willie Winkie? We're not trespassing. . . .'

'Yet,' Piers qualified, panting in fear.

'Look, it's perfectly safe,' I reassured him as we approached the last lap of our little walkies. 'It's perfectly safe. She's flown to Washington for the unveiling of President Reagan's new nose.'

Piers hung back, whimpering, 'Suppose we bump into someone else. . . .?'

I propelled him round the corner. 'At this time of night?' I asked, as we bumped into a lurking Police Constable on Security Duty.

The policeman barred our way with one hand, the other fondling his holster. 'Where do you think you gentlemen are going?' he inquired loftily.

'We're not going to the Prime Minister's Office, if that's what you're thinking. . . .' I tweaked Piers's scrotum which shut him up.

'It's quite all right, Officer,' I retrieved the situation with urbanity. 'We're just taking a stroll, drinking in the historic ambience. . . .'

The policeman relaxed his guard and stated reasonably, 'I'll have to ask you to identify yourselves, sir. Several ministerial offices on this floor; can't be too careful. . . .'

'I quite understand,' I said agreeably, searching my pockets for my I.D. Piers produced his House of Commons library card. Luckily I found a cutting from *The Telegraph* about the Gun Law, with my photograph on it.

'You're Alan Bastard?' The policeman stepped back in respect.

'B'Stard,' I corrected him.

'You're the Member who got that Bill through arming us police, aren't you?' He recollected and drew himself up to full attention in respect.

'Indeed, I'm proud to say that was I,' I confirmed. 'It wasn't easy, but I felt you chaps deserved the tools to do the job.'

'Oh, I'm a big fan of yours, sir,' the policeman said with awe, wiping his right palm on his thigh and extending it to me. 'If I shook you by the hand would it be a terrible liberty?'

'Yes it would . . . but just this once,' I shook his hand and put my left arm round Piers's shoulders to stop him shuffling his feet on the marble floor in nervousness like a small boy who had to pee. I pushed Piers forward, saying, 'This is Piers Fletcher-Dervish, who helped draft the Bill. Probably the sharpest legal brain in this corridor at the moment,' I said without exaggeration.

'It's a real pleasure, sir.' The policeman bowed to Piers and almost clicked his heels.

'Is it?' Piers asked, bewildered, as he allowed his hand to be pumped.

'Tell me, Officer, do you find the gun makes a great deal of difference to your work?' I asked him with professional interest.

'A revelation, sir,' he nodded, and leaned toward me confidentially. 'Take last Saturday. A mate of mine in the Met was policing the Chelsea match. Some hooligan throws a bottle on to the pitch, so he draws his piece and blows him all over the half-time scoreboard. Splat!'

'Eugh!' Piers shuddered as the policeman chuckled. 'Wasn't no trouble after that, sir. Yes, you've done us Bobbies a right favour,' he nodded. 'I mean, in this day and age, what good's a truncheon? Though the wife likes it, mind, when I'm on nights.' Through Piers' tittering, the officer explained, 'Something to grab hold of if she thinks she hears an intruder. . . .'

'Officer, since we're such kindred spirits, I wonder if you could do us a small favour,' I inquired, getting down to the business at hand.

The policeman saluted me, saying deferentially, 'If I can, sir.'

'Actually,' I confided. 'It's Mr Fletcher-Dervish, here. He's never been into a Minister's room, and, unlike me, he's never likely to get the opportunity.' I gently pushed Piers into the centre of our little group, continuing to plead his cause, 'Could you let him have a peek in one of the offices? Needn't be anything grand. Agriculture, Fish and Food; Northern Ireland even. . . .'

'Well, I don't know, sir,' the officer replied, to Piers's all too visible relief. 'I shouldn't leave my post.'

'I'll keep an eye out for you,' I offered solemnly.

'All right, Mr B'Stard, as it's you,' the policeman conceded with a wink, and took the hapless Piers off down the corridor, pointing out to him, 'This here's the office of the Chancellor of the Duchy of Lancaster, whatever that is, this broom cupboard used to be Lord Palmerston's khazi.'

As the policeman's voice faded away I slipped across the corridor in silence and tried the brass handle on the door marked Prime Minister's Office. Miraculously, the door swung open on well-oiled hinges. Crossing the darkened antechamber, I entered the office. I whistled softly to light the handy little torch on the Bentley's key ring and removed my Swiss Army knife from my other pocket.

The filing cabinet was securely locked, but the catch on the Prime Minister's desk drawer sprang easily, but with a click that nearly frightened me out of my skin. Trembling, I riffled through the drawer's contents. Beneath a framed, autographed photo of Cecil Parkinson and a copy of *Spycatcher* I found just what I was looking for. I removed three sheets of notepaper bearing the PM's crest and relocked the drawer in silence. Folding the stationery neatly in my breast pocket, I flicked off the torch and tiptoed back into the corridor, snicking the door shut as quietly as I could. I was back at my station coolly guarding the officer's beat and humming merrily to myself a good thirty seconds before he returned a profusely sweating and obviously grateful Piers to my care and control.

I sent Piers up to the Smoking Room for half an hour to partake of some late evening jolly japes with Sir Stephen and all the other boring old duffers who frequent the place, and nipped back up to my office to compose the letter that would bring Ocelot to its knees. My masterpiece went:

Dear Sir Adrian,

My Cabinet and I were gratified to receive your personal assurances this afternoon that you and your Board of Directors have decided to fall in line with our proposed Policy for Industrial efficiency for the next budgetary year and will proceed forthwith to operate your works in such a manner as to guarantee that its output will be trebled within the next six months, so that Ocelots can begin to compete in price and quality with Japanese and other foreign cars both on the home market and throughout the world, including the Soviet Union.

For the record, my Government fully supports the proposal of the Board of Ocelot Motors to de-unionise their factories and reduce wages by thirty per cent to ensure price competitiveness into the next decade.

With the assurance of continued best wishes to yourself and to your charming wife, Lady Arabella, I remain

Yours sincerely,
Margaret Thatcher
Prime Minister

I ruined one precious piece of the PM's stationery by typing in today's date. I smacked my forehead and rolled another sheet of crested notepaper into the typewriter, dating it a week earlier when I remembered Maggie had been entertaining the Soviet Ambassador to tea and *glasnost* at Number Ten that afternoon.

Using the tippex only twice, I rapidly typed the letter and was signing it with an illegible pp when Piers entered the office, lit cigar and full brandy snifter in hand. He appeared much more relaxed, almost devil-may-care.

I had to dangle the inducement of a Supercat in front of Piers's greedy nose only twice more to persuade him to agree to his part of the bargain.

I filched an unidentifiable piece of paper from Sir Stephen's desk, put the paper on the blotter on Piers's desk and sat him down before it, placing a blue biro in his left hand.

As I dictated, Piers scrawled:

Dear Mr Crippen,
Sometimes I volunteer for unpaid overtime as I was so happy in my job as a tea lady in the Ocelot Motors works canteen. Today I was clearing up the tea things in the bored room after a meeting when what should I find on the table bold as brass but the inclosed letter from Maggie to our Guvnor.

I think it is a disgrace I said to the foreman who said I should send it to you as you are are MP and have got are intrests at steak. I voted for you by the by.

You will know what to do with it he said. I say Ocelot and England are depending on you.

We look forward to hearing from you soonest.

Yours faithfully,
   A. Constituent (Mrs.)

I neatly folded the two letters into an envelope which Piers addressed in the same hand to Comrade Bob c/o the House of Commons. Slapping a first-class stamp on it, I handed the envelope back to Piers to post from Bramall the next day.

Everything went according to plan and two days later pandemonium reigned in the House. I relaxed in my seat and enjoyed it, attempting to conceal my smile as Bob Crippen swallowed the bait, hook, line and sinker.

'I don't care how many times the Minister denies it, I've got it here in black and white, on the Prime Minister's own notepaper,' Comrade Bob waved the letter in the air, then recited its contents to the assembled House. There was more barking and braying going on in the House than I'd ever heard before. It sounded like feeding time at the zoo.

The Secretary of State for Employment leapt to his feet and expostulated, 'I don't know where the honourable Member for Bramall obtained this ludicrous misinformation. . . .'

Face red with indignation, Crippen shouted, 'I'm not telling you, pal! But I'm sure I speak for all Members on this side of the House when I demand a full public inquiry!' He banged his fist on the back of the bench in front of him, whose occupant ducked for cover.

'Order! Order!', the Speaker bellowed.

'Despite the Tory Government's sinister and undemocratic attempt to sweep this scandal under the carpet, it is my duty to lift that carpet and find other scandals from previous carpets,' Crippen banged on as my heart began to sink.

I leaned over and poked Piers in the ribs, whispering, 'No, not a Public Inquiry! That'll take at least ten years, Piers; this isn't going badly enough!'

'Do I get a choice of colours?' Piers muttered, immersed in the copy of *Yuppie Car* that he'd hidden in his Order Papers. 'I fancy a black one. . . .' 'What?' 'My new Ocelot Supercat.'

'Oh shut up and shout "Outrageous" Piers.' 'Outrageous Piers' The dolt bellowed obediently.

Meanwhile, Crippen ground self-righteously on.

'. . . but some public-spirited employee of Ocelot has had the decency to leak this letter to me and I will not betray their solidarity!' Crippen swore, shaking his fist.

'Order! Order!' the Speaker admonished again. I leaped to my feet. 'B'Stard,' he acknowledged me.

Crippen growled, 'I will briefly yield to the Honourable Member for Haltemprice, because it's always enlightening to listen to the crypto-fascist ravings of the loony right. Though I doubt if even he can find a way to justify this scandalous conspiracy.'

'*Au contraire*, Mr Speaker, which I translate as "That's what you think" for the benefit of the Member for Bramall, who probably never went to school,' I began, to Tory cheers, 'I'm sure all of us on this side of the House are sick and tired of this typical lefty Trot whingeing! It's not as if the average car worker has the taste and intelligence to spend his outrageously high pay packet on anything more worthwhile than pigeons, whippets, brown ale and oven-ready chips,' I stated with disdain to more 'hear, hear's' from my side of the floor.

Crippen was now well and truly wound up. He shouted, 'Outrageous! I myself am a member of the National Union of Car Workers and I have the privilege to represent that body in this august chamber and because of him,' he stressed, pointing his finger across the House at me, 'I demand that the executive committee recommend a private ballot for industrial action to be taken if the scumbag opposite does not withdraw those outrageous slanders.'

As Crippen's side raised this voices in unanimous support of him, I continued to goad him with, ' "Industrial action!", Mr Crippen's answer to everything. Here we are dealing with a man whose family history shows he was related to a very dubious member of the medical profession!

That did it. Crippen leaped to his feet, proclaiming, 'Right, that's it! I shall call for a national strike of all car workers in Britain if B'Stard doesn't withdraw that vicious slander.'

'Keep your hair on, Crippen!' I shouted back.

'Please! Order! Order!' the Speaker instructed, but the House took no notice.

'You're dead, pal!' Crippen hurled at me above the uproar.

I sat down, satisfied, I whispered to Piers, 'I think that's done the trick.'

Sarah spent the first month of the ensuing strike at the Gidleigh-Park family seat, a mouldering old pile on the outskirts of the village. She refused to speak to me, using Roland and Beatrice Protheroe as intermediaries. It didn't seem worthwhile dragging myself to Haltemprice and back for weekends, what with no hot meals laid on, so I spent the weeks at my Flood Street *pièd a terre*, mostly taking r. and r. at my favourite club, Stringfellows, bopping and boffing 'til I nearly dropped. It was no real hardship, as I had plenty of opportunity to catch a few catnaps during Debates.

By the fifth week, Ocelot shares had spiralled so far downwards that Sarah phoned me at the flat and adopted a semi-civil tone. She said she was moving back to Haltemprice as Ingleborough Manor was far too cold to endure and was I coming home for the weekend, as we needed to talk?

I needed a supply of clean shirts, so I agreed to go up. It was a mistake. Roland and Beatrice rounded on me for stopping Sarah's allowance as soon as I walked through the front door.

'When I get through with you, B'Stard,' Roland thundered, shaking his fist at me, 'the only seat you'll have left is the seat of your pants, and that's if you're lucky, you bastard.'

'It's really most unfortunate they didn't pass the Abortion Act before you were born,' Beatrice chimed in with equal venom, 'My heart goes out to that poor girl. I've had to lend her more than £2000 since you put a stop on her credit cards. After all, a tory M.P.'s wife can't appear to be poverty stricken, you pathetic parliamentary prick.'

'There's loyalty for you,' I sniffed and pushed past them to confront Sarah in the drawing room. She took one look at me, dropped her head into her hands and wept.

'Don't you mess with me, Sweetheart,' I warned her in Bogey-like tones. She began to wail most unbecomingly.

I left my dirty laundry in the kitchen, picked up a dozen fresh shirts from my wardrobe and swept back to London.

I had to do something to speed things up. I had to create a real no-win situation, for everyone but myself, that is.

Early Monday morning I drove up to Bramall in the Bentley, having stopped at Lillywhites at opening time to pick up my disguise. I parked some distance from the Ocelot Motors Factory, donned my balaclava and dufflecoat and went to join the picket at the works' barred gates.

There were only a dozen or so dispirited picketers stamping their feet in the cold and warming their hands over the glowing brazier. I joined them, removing my gloves and rubbing my hands together over the coals.

'Happen the management was telling t'truth . . . ? One picket asked the rest of the group.

'The letter were on't Prime Minister's own bloody writing paper,' another assured them

'Listen,' a third picket said. 'Stand further away from me. I haven't had a square meal for five weeks and I'm bloody hungry!'

'Food, huh,' I chipped in over the growling of his stomach.

'You're a disgrace to t'memory of Tolpuddle Martyrs! We've been out five weeks now, another few months and the management will cave in, you mark my words,' I tapped my blazing hot finger to my nose and declared in a broad Yorkshire accent. 'But go back and we'll be on coolie wages for t'rest of our working lives! Now, cheer bloody up, and who's for a fish supper, on me?'

The pickets raised their hands to a man, I loped off, promising them over my shoulder, 'I'll not be long.'

Ocelot shares nosedived that very afternoon. I decided to nip home the following day to effect the reconciliation. On my terms, of course.

Sarah was angrily ripping up brochures of exotic holidays and homes and dropping them into the waste bin in the drawing room when I arrived. I poured myself a brandy and inquired in a placatory manner, 'Can I get you a drink, darling?'

She didn't respond. 'Some warm olive oil to syringe your ears?' I offered.

'I heard what you said,' Sarah grunted.

'Good, in that case, tell me, are you still going through with the divorce,' I asked, getting straight down to business.

'How can I, now that my Ocelot shares have been devalued by ninety-seven percent by a vicious strike that co-incidentally started immediately after you found out I was going to leave you?' She snarled and hurled the rest of the brochures into the bin.

'Sarah, surely you can't believe an ordinary backbencher could foment a major strike to save his marriage?' I asked her in outraged shock.

'You're not an ordinary backbencher,' Ssarah declared, grabbing my drink and draining it.

'True,' I agreed as I poured myself another drink. 'And I admit I do love you enough to do anything in my power to stop you from divorcing me. . . .'

'You don't love me! You don't love anyone except yourself,' Sarah hollered like a common fishwife. 'All you want is to keep your rotten seat in Parliament. That's what you need me for!'

'Sarah, darling, why so bitter?' I attempted to appease her. 'I admit I made a silly mistake with a secretary! She was a temp, and I was tempted. I'm only human,' I admitted. 'But that's history now, Let's put it behind us and go forward together to a brighter tomorrow.'

I put my arms around her, but she shrugged me off, saying, 'You don't know the difference between a declaration of love and a Party political broadcast,' she went on, baring her tiny little teeth. 'All right, you've won. I'm not divorcing you; but that doesn't mean I want to have anything to do with you ever again!'

'But that's not good enough, Sarah. A politician, especially a Tory politician, needs his wife at his side at key moments in his career. It's not a lot to ask,' I said reasonably. 'If Joan Kennedy was prepared to help Teddy run for President when they hadn't spoken for five years, I'm bloody sure you can stand next to me at the odd constituency do . . .'

'Give me one reason!' she snarled at me disagreeably.

'I'll double your allowance . . .' I offered, simply to clinch the deal.

Sarah decided this was the moment to give in gracefully.

'I suppose I ought to give you another chance. Marriage should be worked at, after all,' she irrationalised as she slumped back on to the sofa.

'I know, and I'll try to come home more at weekends so we can spend those precious days together,' I conceded sweetly.

'I'd rather you didn't, Alan. Just remember the allowance . . . and I don't know whether I've ever told you this, but I've always rather fancied a yacht . . .' Sarah let the sentence dangle, really pressing her luck.

We settled on a two-week holiday in Barbados. I insisted she take Beatrice as a chaperone as I still didn't trust her completely ever since she'd mentioned that mysterious lover. Thoroughly cowed, she rapidly agreed and I drove back to Westminster, victorious.

Even Victoria's abortion couldn't burst my balloon, I felt on top of the world again. After all, I had shares in the clinic. The following afternoon I was interviewing a smashing new temp. I leaned back in my seat and eyed her shapely legs as she perched on my desk. I impressed her with my huge majority and went on to discuss my stenographic needs. I leaned towards her and confided, 'Yes, our last secretary got pregnant, so we had to let her go. Unfortunately, there isn't a crêche in the House, otherwise Piers would be in it,' I quipped in a friendly fashion, patting her knee.

I blew Annette a little kiss as she exited.

'Seen the *Financial Times* today?' Piers asked, not concealing his triumph as he handed me the pink paper.

'Of course,' I said, pushing it away.

'Stock exchange has suspended dealings in Ocelot shares. I don't suppose Sarah will be divorcing you now?' he inquired, but not idly.

'No, she won't. So what?' I replied, my mind on Annette across the Square.

Piers frowned. 'You said you'd get me a black Ocelot Supercat if I helped you,' he complained.

'And you believed me?' I replied in wonderment at his credulity.

'Did at the time,' Piers admitted. 'I supposed I'm just really very stupid . . .'

'Yes you are, Piers,' I declared. 'Stupid but loyal. Follow me.' I ordered.

I led Piers to the underground carpark. There, beside my Bentley, was a gorgeous, gleaming white Supercat.

'There she is,' I announced in hushed tones.

'It's beautiful,' Piers gasped. 'Thank you Alan . . . .'

'I'm sorry I couldn't get a black one, but there aren't many around at the moment,' I apologised as Piers ran a loving hand over the Supercat's paintwork.

'Go on. Get in and try it for size,' I urged him.

Piers attempted to open the Supercat's doors but couldn't find his way in. 'The door won't open, Alan,' he said, bewildered.

I removed the electronic key from my pocket and aimed it at the Supercat's gullwing doors. They lifted gently as I pressed the remote control button.

'Oh, Alan,' Piers drew in his breath sharply. 'You really didn't have to, you know. . . .'

'Of course I did, Piers. After all, you've been my loyal and faithful servant. It's the least I could do,' I declared, squeezing his arm.

Piers settled into the Supercat's driving seat and I pressed the remote control again to shut the gullwing doors. Piers happened upon the button that opened the driver's window. 'I just don't know how to thank you, Alan,' he said as he started up the engine.

'Don't thank me,' I raised my voice to be heard above the engine's gentle purr. 'Thank Hertz. I gave them your credit card number. You can settle up with them when you take it back. It's £150 a day or £975 for the week. . . .'

The Supercat lurched backward as Piers screamed out of the window at me, 'You're a bastard, Alan!'

I saluted him. 'B'Stard, Piers.' I corrected and walked off towards the exit, roaring with laughter. I have to say that the echo in the car park made me sound quite diabolical.

CHAPTER THREE

SEX IS WRONG

It was a week before the Conservative Party Conference in Blackpool. I always enjoy these knees-up because it brings me closer to the people. Actually, to be perfectly honest, it brings me closer to one of the people: my Agent, Beatrice, the one woman I've ever met who is a real match for me. She's so feminine, so frilly, but underneath that deceptively soft, sensitive exterior, which is the position I'd been aiming to get in for at least three years, lurks a wit and intelligence almost equal to mine.

I was sure that Beatrice had the hots for me, too. All the signs were there: she had contrived to spend an increasing amount of time with Sarah and me in Haltemprice, she would blush charmingly whenever I entered the room and found her whiling away the time with my wife, obviously awaiting my electric presence. The more she denied it, the more it seemed true and I just couldn't wait finally to break down her natural reserve and shag her silly.

Beatrice had come down to London for the day to go over what I was expected to do and time was ripe for a dress rehearsal.

'. . . your constituency association has tabled a motion about privatisation, so you will be expected to make a speech,' she declared as I backed her up against the office bookcase and slid my hand up her thigh. 'And will you please take your hand out from under my skirt?'

'Beatrice! I admonished gently, my hand still creeping up her leg. 'Why are you so hard on yourself? Why can't you admit you want me?'

Beatrice slapped at my hand through her hiked-up skirt. She exclaimed professionally, 'Alan, try to concentrate on the matter in hand!'

'I love it when you talk dirty,' I whispered as I removed my hand from her leg to run my fingers lightly down her spine through her silk blouse.

Beatrice shivered and reached behind her back to withdraw my hand, admitting, 'I'm attracted to you, Alan, of course I am.'

'Who isn't,' I agreed and kissed her neck.

'But it would never work!' Beatrice pushed me away with a scowl. 'What about Sarah?'

'Sarah?' I asked stupidly. All the blood had rushed from my brain to a different part of my anatomy.

'Yes, my old school friend. You must remember Sarah; you're married to her,' she said as I resumed my embrace.

I clasped her to my chest, declaring, 'Oh Sarah. She'd be relieved if she knew we were having an affair. She's never been interested in sex, frigid cow!' I pulled Beatrice down to the floor, saying urgently, 'Not like you. Come on, let's do it now, under the desk!'

Piers blundered into the office as we were groping and grappling on the carpet. 'I say, have you seen the Whip?'

Beatrice panted as she slithered out from under the desk and exited from the office in one embarrassed bound, exclaiming over her shoulder, 'Bless you, Piers.'

'But I didn't sneeze,' Piers called out to Beatrice's retreating form.

I gnashed my teeth and stood up, brushing the carpet fluff from my Gieves and Hawks suit. 'You mean you aren't ill? How depressing.' I sat down at my desk, staring daggers at him.

'Was I interrupting something?' Piers asked innocently.

'No, no. You're as welcome as Jeffrey Archer at the *Daily Star* Christmas Party,' I groaned.

'Oh, that's all right then,' Piers said happily as he sat down at his desk.

'I thought you were visiting Sir Stephen in hospital?' I said, checking my watch.

'I was,' Piers confirmed with a nod. 'But I didn't want to stay too long. The old chap was feeling very weak and weary.'

'So he's back to normal,' I joshed.

Piers looked at me blankly. 'Not quite, but he's planning to discharge himself tomorrow. . . .'

'After a prostate operation? That'll be a medical first!'

'I'm sorry, I don't understand.' Piers frowned.

'It's not your fault, Piers, it's the centuries of inbreeding,' I reassured him. Piers looked so hurt that I decided to change the subject.

'So, have you found yourself a pretty little bedwarmer for the Party Conference?' I asked in a confidential manner as I reseated myself on the edge of his desk.

'What do you mean?' Piers asked, cocking his head and drawing his eyebrows together.

I bragged, 'Beatrice was just inviting me to share her suite at the Imperial Hotel . . . .'

'Why? Are you on a diet?' Piers interrupted obtusely.

'Her hotel suite,' I stressed, banging Piers's desk. 'God, if your IQ was any lower you'd need watering.'

'Are you talking about illicit sex?' Piers rocked back in his chair in astonishment.

'Yes, yes, illicit sex. The best sort!' I replied heartily and waggled my tongue suggestively.

'Alan,' Piers rose to his feet and confronted me. 'It's not normal for a man to chase after every woman he sees. Homo Sapiens is naturally – he groped – monogamous.' He shook his head at me in disapproval.

' "Naturally monogamous," ' I mocked. 'Where are you getting all those five guinea words? Anything more than two syllables and you usually have to lie down.'

'Well,' Piers began excitedly, 'you know Sir Stephen's the Chairman of the Campaign for Moral Regeneration. . . . ?'

'No, I didn't know, but it makes sense.' I began to tell Piers a few sad facts of life. 'It's a fine old English tradition; when you're too decrepit to do it, you start a committee to stop other people doing it. . . .'

'How dare you?' Piers overspilled with righteous indignation. 'Sir Stephen and Lady Rosemary have been happily married for forty-seven years,' he exclaimed.

'Happily?' I humphed. 'Then why is he lying in hospital minus his prostate?' I tapped him on the shoulder with my pointed finger and stressed, 'I'll tell you why: lack of use! Well, I'm not letting mine go rusty!'

He sat down rubbing his shoulder and stared at me in silent shock. A second later he declared gravely, 'You're morally bankrupt, Alan.' He shook his head at me in despair.

I snorted, 'That's rich, coming from someone whose father was convicted of sheep worrying.'

Piers lowered his eyes to his desk and said, 'It wasn't Daddy's fault. It was regimental tradition.'

'Then why did he ask for seventeen other animals to be taken into account?' I hooted as I sat down and plopped my legs on the desk in triumph. 'Baa, Baaaa,' bleated. I just love to taunt Piers.

'Yes, pour scorn. That's what you always do.' Piers slapped his desk in anger. 'I don't care. Our once great nation is reeling under a vicious onslaught of filth and pornography, Sir Stephen said. And it's up to us to do something about it!' he cried heartily.

I mimed a yawn. 'You don't mean you've joined this absurd campaign?' I asked with idle incredulity.

'Yes,' Piers affirmed with pride.

'But they'll all be repressed, blue-rinsed old virgins in K-Skips and support hose . . . and the woman are worse,' I said slowly, attempting to make the poor clot see sense.

Piers went on with dogged determination. 'There's a Campaign meeting tomorrow afternoon. You really ought to attend, for your own good. . . .'

'Oh no, you're not roping me in! I'm a libertarian!' I swung my legs to the floor and stood up, declaring, 'If there's a demand for pornography, and people prepared to fulfil it, then who are we to interfere with the market mechanism. That's the slippery road to socialism!'

Piers grabbed me earnestly by the lapels. 'If you really believe that, then there's no more to say,' he announced.

'Good,' I said, shrugging him off and moving to look out of the window at the passing typists.

'Good,' Piers repeated, having the last word. He paused for a second and then continued his diatribe, 'But I'm sure that if you saw the sort of obscene films we have to sit through at Campaign meetings, you'd be as disgusted as I am. . . .'

I turned from the window and tipped my head towards Piers in interest. 'Filthy films?'

'Awful vile films!' Piers acknowledged with a vehement nod. 'Tomorrow we're going to have to endure "Snow White and the Seven Perverts". It makes me shudder just to think of it.'

I rummaged through my desk drawer for my filofax. 'What time tomorrow?'

Piers smiled with pride as I entered the committee room the following afternoon. He gestured to the seat next to him, which he'd reserved for me with a sign saying 'Reserved for A B'Stard' written in his own childish, rounded handwriting. He needn't have bothered. Only four braying middle-aged women and seven clapped-out, balding fuddy-duddy gentlemen dotted the extensive rows of empty chairs. I settled myself in beside Piers, the only other young member of this motley crowd. From the Chair, Sir Stephen smiled a wan welcome at me and gestured for the lights to be switched off. Piers sprang to his feet to perform his task as Sir Stephen aimed his remote control thingy at the television and the video began to play.

I sat in rigid attention for the forty-five minutes the flick lasted. Judging by the rustlings engendered by the almost compulsive crossing and uncrossing of varicoid legs from the other so-called men, the rest of the audience also found the film attention-grabbing if not exactly uplifting.

'Well, there you have it,' Sir Stephen cleared his throat, spitting out, ' "Snow White and the Seven Perverts" '.

Someone near the door switched on the lights and we all blinked and stretched, still hushed with shock.

'To think I left my sick bed for this,' Sir Stephen mustered up his strength to exclaim in anger. 'There are no words to express my abhorrence of this hateful film . . . but if there are any comments?'

Piers lurched to his feet. 'Excuse me, Sir Stephen, but on a point of information,' he inquired, brows knitted. 'I haven't seen "Snow White" since Nanny took me to the Devizes Gaumont, Christmas 1961, I think, but I'm sure there wasn't really a dwarf called "Nobby." Was there?'

He was forced to sit down unanswered amid jeers of 'Oh, sit down! Shut up, Fletcher-Dervish!'

'Any other observations?' Sir Stephen asked the audience who answered him with silence. 'Good. Then I think this is the opportunity to break for a cup of good honest tea to get the taste of decadence out of our mouths.' He rose shakily to his feet, signalling the committee to follow him into the antechamber, and announced, 'We'll reconvene in twenty minutes to examine the pornographic photographs kindly lent by the Metropolitan Police Commissioner from his personal collection.' The audience gasped collectively. He turned at the doorway and Sir

Stephen, corrected himself, 'I'm sorry, I mean lent by the Commissioner from the Metropolitan Police's collection. Twenty minutes then,' he reminded us in more robust tones.

As the committee filed out in Sir Stephen's wake I lagged behind, curious to examine the folder of photographs to which Sir Stephen had alluded at first hand. I found the well-thumbed folder behind the television. One glance through its truly mind-blowing contents convinced me I could gain more profit from it than the Committee for the Campaign for Moral Regeneration possibly could.

In the solitude of my office a few minutes later I examined the photographs more closely, with an editorial eye. They were certainly diverse and included permutations of people with other people and people with animals. A snake? Even I couldn't have had had the colourful imagination to dream that one up, I was sitting happily sorting out the animal pix, trying to get some zingy animal husbandry book proposal together in my mind, when my phone rang.

'Alan B'Stard, rising star of the new right,' I chirped into the receiver. 'Oh Norman.' I listened carefully to his latest money-spinning wheeze. 'What? Ten thousand copies actually signed by Peter Wright. Well, it sounds like a very interesting investment opportunity. How much?' Norman reeled off a five-figure sum. 'I'm sure it's a bargain,' I agreed, 'but I've only just completed the last payment on the massage parlour and I don't have fifty thousand pounds to rub together.' As I paused to estimate how much capital I would need to use on my own new publishing venture, a tentative knock on the door sounded. I ignored it, telling Norman, 'I suppose I could sell some of Sarah's jewels. . . .'

A more robust burst of knocks sounded. 'Look, I've got to go,' I said, hanging up. I stuffed the photos in my desk drawer, trilling, 'Come in.'

A faded suburban flower of about forty tentatively entered the office.

'Here you are, Miss,' her police escort tipped his helmet at her and left.

I looked her up and down quizzically. 'Do I know you?'

'We've never met,' the woman acknowledged, and explained. 'I wrote to you. I'm a constituent.'

'Ah, then I'm afraid there's been a misunderstanding. I don't talk to constituents,' I stated my policy, waving her to the door.

'You did invite me to see you, Sir Stephen,' she said, standing her ground and handing me a letter, which I perused with sudden interest. What was in this for me? If nothing I could always plead misunderstanding. I could pretend my name was Piers Fletcher-Dervish.

'Lady Virginia,' I apologised, kissing her hand. 'I'm so sorry, pressure of work. Forgive me. And do sit down,' I said, making her comfortable in my visitor's chair, I sat down behind my desk again, glanced once more at the letter, then gave her my full and respectful attention. 'Now, you wrote to me about publishing a book of yours?'

'Yes,' Lady Virginia confirmed, and added, 'Must say I thought you'd be older.'

I examined my nails in a modest fashion and agreed, 'Yes, people do say I have a wisdom and gravity that belies my youth.' I leaned forward, placing my hand on my chin, and continued in a business-like tone, 'Now, tell me about your book.'

Lady Virginia shrugged, 'Hardly a book, just a pamphlet really.' She took a brown envelope from her handbag and handed it to me.

I removed the manuscript from the envelope and read, ' "Sex is Wrong". Arresting title,' I conceded. What a nutcase. Trust Sir Stephen to come to the aid of this spinster of his parish.

'Thank you,' Lady Virginia acknowledged my praise. 'Of course, I don't mean sex is wrong in all circumstances. For the purpose of procreating the human race within the sanctity of holy wedlock, I suppose it's permissible,' she elucidated, twisting her lace hankie in her hands.

'Yes, I'm sure,' I calmed her. 'And you were hoping I could help you get your little pamphlet published?' I encouraged her to continue.

'You said you'd try . . . in your letter, as Chairman of the Campaign,' she replied, overcome with nerves again.

'Yes, yes of course,' I assured her with a robust smile. 'As it happens, I've recently joined the board of a little publishing house, dedicated to producing morally uplifting works. I'm sure I could persuade them to issue a limited edition of your essay. . . .'

'That's wonderful, Sir Stephen,' Lady Virginia exclaimed. Her faded blue eyes lit with animation and a flush rose to her scrawny neck.

'Yes, it is, isn't it?' I concurred. 'However, they are a non-profit making charitable foundation, and, as such, I'm afraid it's necessary for the author to make a nominal contribution to the printing costs,' I qualified the deal. From her moniker and from her well-cut tweed suit I could tell the lady was loaded.

'I quite understand,' Lady Virginia responded reasonably.

'Shall we say, seventy-five pence a copy and a print run of two thousand?' I tried it on.

'Yes, all right. That sounds most reasonable,' Lady Virginia nodded. She reached across the desk to shake my hand.

'Good,' I purred, taking her damp palm in mine. 'And if we hurry, we may have your booklet ready for sale at the Conservative Party Conference,' I added as a bonus.

'Oh, how splendid!' Lady Virginia crowed, then continued ruefully, 'I can't attend the Conference myself. I'm rather phobic where crowds are concerned.

'Oh good, er – grief, what a pity. Now, I suppose the best

thing is if you let me have a cheque. . . .'

'What, right away?' she questioned the procedure.

'No time to lose, my dear,' I replied as she withdrew a Coutts chequebook from her bag.

'I'm in your hands,' Lady Virginia acknowledged politely as she uncapped her fountain pen. 'Payable to Sir Stephen Baxter?'

'Goodness no, of course not!' I put my hand over my heart feigning shock. 'You must make it out to the charity and the charity is. . . .' I thought quickly. ' "Christian Approach to Society Handbooks".'

Lady Virginia frowned at her cheque. 'I don't think I can squeeze that all in,' and began to write.

I stopped her writing hand with a smooth motion. 'Yes, it is a bit of a mouthful, I'm afraid. Just the initials then,' I conceded, letting go of her hand.

Lady Virginia completed the cheque and handed it to me. 'Pay C.A.S.H. One thousand five hundred pounds.' I approved it. 'Perfect.'

She put her pen and chequebook back into her handbag and stood. I led her gallantly to the door, 'Now, if you'll excuse me, there's no time to lose. You don't mind showing yourself out, do you? There's a policeman outside who will show you the street.' I pushed her gently out of the door, which I closed after her.

Fearing that any moment Sir Stephen and Piers would interrupt me, I sped back to my desk and quickly dialed my contact, I got through in seconds. 'Hello, Horniman Press? This is Mr . . . Alan here. Yes, that's right, the publisher of *Big Wobblers*', I confirmed, and asked rapidly, 'Can you do me a rush job? Well, it's a sort of religious tract, but with some rather unusual illustrations.' I had to laugh at the next question. 'Are they hot? Let's just say I'll be sending you the photos in an asbestos envelope!'

I'd promised to deliver the typescript and photos later in the afternoon and repaired to the Smoking Room to await Sir Stephen and Piers, who'd need a couple of stiff drinks after the blue film.

' "Children who develop a morbid interest in their private parts should have their hands bound at bedtime. . . ." This is not the work of a well woman,' I shook my head sadly as I reached my favourite table, which was already occupied by an old Labour duffer wearing a battered suit and crumpled face. I sat down and said to him pointedly, 'This is a Tory table. Labourites sit over there, in the draught.' I gestured across the room. The man didn't respond. 'Are you deaf?' I complained, annoyed. 'Oh, you are,' I said as I spied his hearing aid. There was nothing for it. His smouldering pipe was resting in the ashtray. I picked it up and popped it, sizzling, into his pint. The Socialist took the hint and scurried across the floor.

Piers and Sir Stephen were just entering the Smoking Room, looking depressed and conspiratorial. I gestured them to my table, 'Over here. Sit down, Sir Stephen, mustn't overtire yourself,' He sank gingerly into the seat I pulled out for him. 'Drink?' I offered solicitously.

'Yes, thank you. . . .'

'Large Wincarnis?' The old boy certainly looked as if he needed building up.

Sir Stephen waved away my suggestion. 'No, I need something stronger. Think I'll have a double Scotch and ginger ale. . . .'

'And I'll have a large Armagnac, please, Piers.' I turned my winning smile on Piers, who was about to sit down.

'What?' Piers looked confused.

'It's your round,' I pointed out patiently.

'Oh, of course. Sorry,' he apologised as he went off to the bar.

Sir Stephen sighed. 'I feel quite distressed after that disgusting film,' he stated.

'Yes,' I sympathised. 'Must have been awful for a man in your condition. Rather like having your stomach removed and then being taken round Harrods' Food Hall.'

Sir Stephen grunted as Piers returned to the table empty-handed as well as empty-brained.

'Where are the drinks, Piers?' I reminded him.

'Oh, drinks. I knew there was something,' he said in a distracted fashion. 'And there defnitely wasn't a dwarf called "Horny". . . .' he reflected aloud.

I shooed Piers back to the bar and said to Sir Stephen in a reverent tone, 'I know you'll find this hard to believe, but in the hour since I left your meeting, I've had a moving spiritual experience.'

'Oh, really,' said Sir Stephen, perking up a bit.

'When I returned to my office this booklet was waiting for me,' I said, handing him the typescript.

He peered down at it through his bifocals 'Virginia Imrie . . . the name rings a distant bell. But fortunately he didn't remember she was one of his constituents. I tapped the typescript with my finger and ventured the prophecy, 'It'll ring bells across the nation in years to come. Church bells!'

Piers returned and set three halves of shandy on the table. Even the usually benign Sir Stephen looked a trifle put out.

'We'd be better off with a performing seal,' I commiserated with him. Shrugging, he lifted his glass.

'Cheers!' Piers toasted us, beaming. He spied the typescript on the table. ' "Sex is Wrong"! That's what my fiancée's always saying,' he babbled happily into his shandy.

Sir Stephen opened the typescript and began to read aloud, ' "Sex without marriage is a mortal sin, yet sex within marriage is the enemy of domestic harmony. . . ." ' He slapped the typescript back on to the table, proclaiming, 'This is a work of genius! She sums up my last forty-seven years in a nutshell.'

'I know it's brilliant!' I concurred, nodding enthusiastically. I leaned forward and began to make my pitch. 'We must find a way to disseminate it!'

'Hear hear!' Sir Stephen seconded. 'We must bring this message of hope to a wider audience.' He was already putty in my hands.

'I know,' Piers tapped his empty head. 'Why don't we run off some photocopies?'

I greeted his suggestion with the disdain it deserved. 'Run off some photocopies! Shame on you, Piers. When Moses went up on to Mount Sinai to receive the Ten Commandments, he didn't say, "Cheers, Lord, I'll run off a few photocopies",' I simpered in Piers's own stupid voice. 'No, he went and wrote the Bible, the greatest book in the history of . . . er . . . books. We must give "Sex is Wrong" the best presentation we can afford!'

'You mean we should send it to a publisher?' Sir Stephen asked, downing the rest of his shandy.

'No, I mean we, the Campaign for Moral Regeneration, should publish it ourselves!'

Sir Stephen gazed into his empty glass, considering my suggestion. 'But wouldn't that be frighteningly expensive?' he eventually protested.

'Not necessarily,' I assured him. 'I've taken the liberty of telephoning some printers; and one very old-established firm, specialising in devotional tracts, say they can deliver two thousand bound copies next week at a pound apiece.'

'Ahh!' Sir Stephen interjected, looking at me with respect.

'And,' I continued, 'to prove my sincerity, I'm prepared to pay half the publishing costs. . . .'

'Bravo!' Sir Stephen ejaculated.

Piers got out his pocket calculator and did a quick sum. 'But half of two thousand pounds is point 0004321,' he stated.

'Well done, Chancellor,' I said, taking his calculator and dropping it in his Shandy. 'Now, if the Campaign for Moral Regeneration will put up the other half,' I suggested.

'Of course we will!' Sir Stephen exclaimed excitedly, withdrawing his chequebook from his inside breast pocket. 'To whom should I make the cheque payable?'

'They're called Christian Approach to Society Handbooks, but if you can't squeeze it all on the line, just put in the initials,' I said with an accommodating smile. 'Now, what are you doing to contribute, Piers?'

'I've got a biro,' he held the pen out to Sir Stephen.

'I see, the grand gesture!' I said and flicked the pen across the room. 'Then do you think you could at least exert your sluggish and ungenerous form and run this over to the printers?' I slipped the typescript in with the naughty pix and sealed the envelope with some sealing wax I'd brought along for the occasion.

'Oh yes,' Piers said, reaching out his hand to take the packet from me. 'With pleasure.' I pressed his signet ring into the still hot wax and he sped from the bar blowing on his finger and intent on his mission.

On the way up to Blackpool I stopped at Horniman Press to pick up the two thousand bound copies of *Sex is Wrong*. I had the pallett loaded into the boot of the Bentley as I examined Horniman's workmanship. Not bad for forty pence per copy including shrink-wrapping. It really didn't matter much that three of the photos had been printed upside-down, as the positions they depicted were so convoluted anyway, but I wasn't so sure the punters would swallow the fourth, which now featured a donkey suspended in mid-air on its back, held up with superhuman strength by a man standing on his head, features contorted by what could pass for pain. I pointed the errors out to the Accounts Manager, who swiftly knocked £50 off my bill. I paid over a cheque for £750 and continued my trip, mentally ironing out those few sticky patches that still remained in the speech on privatisation I was due to present tomorrow morning.

Speeches were already in full flow when I arrived in the vestibule of the Conference Centre the next morning, after a business breakfast in Beatrice's suite provided by room service. I do find Power Brunches a turn-on, especially in the company of someone with the snap, crackle and pop of the tasty Beatrice, who was definitely going to succumb to my charms tonight, come what might.

I elbowed past the snaking queue of customers for Jeffrey Archer's latest effort and made my way to our own empty stand. What a pathetic attempt at effective merchandising. I thought as Piers gestured towards his display of *Sex is Wrong*, asking me, 'What do you think?'

Piers had stacked the books like a house of cards so that the first customer tempted to purchase a copy would effect an avalanche of books cascading to the floor.

'Not bad,' I said, not to hurt his feelings, and knocked his poxy display over. Piers scrambled to retrieve the books from the floor and we arranged them less precariously. 'That's better,' I approved my handiwork.

'Thank you,' Piers replied as I taped the sales poster I'd carefully lettered the previous evening to the front of the table.

'Ten pounds!' he exclaimed. 'I thought you said the printer charged a pound per book. Does this mean the Campaign will make a profit?'

'I doubt it, not after we deduct transport costs,' I pretended to consider his question.

'But you brought the books up by car!' Piers protested.

'If you were successful enough to own a Bentley, Piers, you'd know how expensive they are to run,' I quashed him with pursed lips.

'Alan,' he asked, holding a copy of the book up to me. 'Why did the printer wrap them in this plastic stuff?'

'To stop them from having babies,' I riposted with a carefree shrug just as Lady Virginia Imrie hove into my view. Oh Lord,

I'll do anything you want, just get me out of this one, I prayed, and whispered out of the corner of my still-smiling mouth, 'Quick, Piers, call me "Sir Stephen".'

'I can't. He's in London. He's had a relapse,' Piers retorted and began to look around for a phone box.

'No,' I corrected him.' Listen, this poor unworldly girl seems to think I'm Sir Stephen.'

'Why?'

'Because I told her I was,' I explained.

'But you're not. . . .' Piers pointed out obtusely.

'Never mind,' I growled and turned my attention to Lady Virginia, who had reached our table. 'Why Lady Virginia, what a pleasant surprise,' I smiled, and shook her hand. 'I thought you weren't coming to the Conference?'

'I wasn't,' Lady Virginia's hand crept nervously to her throat. 'But I decided I had to come and see my book in print.'

'Well, I'll bring a copy to your hotel this evening because the Conference is just about to break for coffee and this vestibule will be swarming with people,' I threatened, quickly recalling her agoraphobia.

'Oh then, perhaps I will hurry along, Sir Stephen,' Lady Virginia said timorously. Good. I took her by the elbow to usher her solicitously from the room.

The tannoy blared, 'Mr Alan B'Stard, Haltemprice.' It was time for my speech, Christ, I thought and propelled Lady Virginia across the room, more quickly stating offhandedly, 'I don't know, people put their names down to speak, and when the moment arrives. . . .'

The sudden apperance of Beatrice quickly put paid to my little deception. 'Alan,' she admonished, 'you're supposed to be speaking.'

' "Alan"?' Lady Virginia gasped as the tannoy called my name again. 'You told me you were Sir Stephen Baxter.'

'Did he?' Beatrice asked, giving me a quizzical frown as Lady

Virginia shrugged off my grip and raced back to the bookstand.

She picked up a copy of *Sex is Wrong* and slit the shrink-wrap with her nail. 'Oh my God!' she gasped.

'Oh my God!' Piers echoed, boggling at the double-page spread she displayed to him. Beatrice took one look and gave a funny little smile. I always knew she was a seething sex-kitten deep down.

They all glared at me accusingly. 'I can explain . . . it's Piers's fault.' I passed the buck just as the tannoy called, 'For the final time, Mr Alan B'Stard, please!'

Lady Virginia clenched her fist at me in a most unladylike fashion as I passed her on the way to the main auditorium. 'Just you wait until I tell Mrs Thatcher about this!' she threatened.

I attempted to calm my nerves and only half-listened to the conclusion of the speech a pretty but obviously tight-arsed Young Conservative was reciting in a trilling voice over a background of loud snores.

'. . . for why should the Royal Family be dependent on state salaries, like common or garden servants? If their ancient lands and rights were restored, they could live with dignity from their rents, as a great feudal family should! That is what I mean by privatising the Monarchy. 'Thank you,' she simpered to a smattering of applause.

The tannoy announced me and I mounted the podium, taking deep breaths. My nerves weren't helped by the sight of Lady Virginia Imrie and Beatrice Protheroe glowing at me from the back. But if the conference responded to my speech as I expected them to, then perhaps I would live to fight another day. I began my pitch with the usual guff: 'Mr Chairman, fellow Conservatives, Norman, Cecil, Jeffrey, before I start I feel I must say, and I'm sure I speak for all of us, how very much I admired the last speaker. A credit to her family, to Conservatism and to private education, for I hazard that she doesn't attend a multi-racial comprehensive in the People's Republic of Brent!'

I paused for applause, then continued with more panache, 'But to the heart of the motion: denationalisation. Now I shall take the liberty of reinterpreting the motion, for when I hear the word "denationalisation", I don't think of the flotation of the ship-building industry. No, I think of the dilution of our national spirit. The very loss of our nationhood,' I stated portentously, tossing back my locks in emphasis.

'And who is behind this loss of nationhood?' I asked the assembled crowd rhetorically. 'Why, the peddlars of pornography. Our once-great nation is threatened with a tidal wave of filth and so it is up to us to shore up our defences with sturdy sea walls, hewn from the rock of our Christian creed.

'But we need guidance in our battle against this tidal wave. Thank God, guidance exists!' I exclaimed, holding up a copy of my book, *Sex is Wrong* by Lady Virginia Imrie. I continued to hold the book aloft for a few moments in silence and then stated, 'This book pulls no punches. Its text is forthright, the full-colour photographs frankly startling in their sexual detail. This is not a book for the weakminded, but if we are to fight the peddlars of filth we must face up to the shocking perversions they purvey.'

I placed the book on the lectern and leaned forward to confide, 'I consider myself a man of the world. Yet there are acts illustrated here in such depraved complexity that they have taken my breath away. And the picture on page seventeen caused me to telephone the RSPCA immediately.'

I lifted the book again and tantalised the crowd by flicking through a few pages. They all leaned forward, hooked. 'And yet for a mere ten pounds and, after all, what is ten pounds to us Tories? A half-decent cigar or a week's social security for a family of gipsies . . . and I know which I'd prefer . . . for a mere ten pounds you can immerse yourself in Lady Virginia's exposé of the lurid technicolour excesses of the enemy within, thereby rearming yourself in preparation for the final battle ahead between good and evil!'

I rocked back on my heels and concluded my oration with, 'Now I know what you're all thinking. Where on earth can I get a copy?' I acknowledged the audience's nods in silence. 'Well, it's on sale in the vestibule now.'

'If you care about Britain, put your hand in your pocket and buy it!' I exhorted them patriotically, to thunderous applause.

I rushed from the auditorium to help Piers. The stampede had already started. We raked in £8,240 by the end of the afternoon.

I went back to my hotel room at seven to put the money in a safe place, shower and peruse the evening papers which had reported my speech. The *Haltemprice Echo* had given me a really splendid write-up, naturally, since I am the largest share holder.

I relaxed in bed in the comfy dressing gown I'd borrowed from the Dorchester Hotel last year, marvelling at *Sex is Wrong* and generally whiling away time until my eight o'clock dinner engagement with Piers, whom I'd persuaded to treat me to a banquet in celebration of my stupendously profitable oration. A knock on the door interrupted my musings. I snapped the book shut and leaped up from the bed, crying, 'Won't be a sec,' as I straightened the bedclothes. To hell with Piers, I thought, I bet that's Beatrice; it's inevitable.

I smoothed down my hair and retied my dressing gown raffishly as I sped to the door, which I opened with a sigh of anticipation.

It was Lady Virginia Imrie.

'Oh!' I acknowledged as I shut the door in her face.

Doggedly, she tapped on the door again. I shrugged. There appeared to be nothing for it but to hear her out and use my natural charm to dissuade her from spilling the beans to Maggie. Plastering a smile on my face, I opened the door to her.

'May I come in?' Lady Virginia asked as she proceeded to enter the room.

I tried to stop her in her tracks with 'You know I'm naked under this bathrobe?'

Lady Virginia smiled at me strangely and replied, 'That's all right, I'm sure I'm perfectly safe with a moral crusader like you, Sir Peter.'

Taking the bull by the horns, I asked her, 'When you said you'd tell Mrs Thatcher, did you actually mean. . . .'

'Yes, I did,' Lady Virginia nodded. 'But I've changed my mind!'

'Have you?' I asked, surprised by her flexible attitude. I beckoned her further into the room, about to offer her a small drink to seal our renewed friendship and trust.

Lady Virginia leaned against the door frame looking flushed. 'You see,' she stated, 'When I saw you up there on the platform making that wonderful speech, filling that hall with moral fervour, I felt a strange desire within me, a longing I'd never felt before.'

She moved toward me in a predatory manner. I stepped backwards, saying, 'Do you think you could be more specific?'

'You must know that you're a very attractive and charismatic man,' she said as she removed one shoe and threw it over her shoulder.

'Yes, I know that,' I replied as her other shoe went flying.

'Don't make me spell it out, Alan,' she purred. 'I know what I want to do is wrong, but I just don't care.' She pulled me to her by my belt.

'Does that mean you don't want your £1,500 back,' I murmured sweetly, perking up.

'No, but it means I intend to get my money's worth,' she whispered as she untied the robe and slipped it off my shoulders. Dropping my dressing gown casually on to the floor, she kicked the door shut behind her and turned off the light.

'I think I've just experienced a sudden swing to the right!' I exclaimed as she devoured my body with kisses.

You can't judge a book by its cover, I thought to myself tritely as she let herself out at around midnight. I was too shagged to search my mind for a more imaginative way of describing the encounter. I fell asleep immediately.

CHAPTER FOUR

WASTE NOT, WANT NOT

It was an unseasonably warm spring Friday and I could feel the perspiration tracking down my back beneath my pinstripped suit as I laboured over my monthly expenses in my cramped, stuffy office. Would Beatrice wear the £150 I'd put down for liquid bribes for the locals at the pub, I pondered? She was becoming increasingly sharp with me over every little thing: sexual frustration, no doubt. I vowed to take her in hand that weekend for her own good, changed the figure to £33.75 and was tapping out the grand total on my pocket calculator when the phone rang.

It was Norman, in a panic, demanding my immediate presence and gabbling shrilly about the winds of change. His change, I was sure. If Norman as a woman was going to react so hysterically to each little crisis, then I could live without her. As my week's business was all but concluded and I could use some fresh air, I agreed, and Norman dictated involved directions to his new office in the East End.

The Big Bang was definitely changing the East End for the better, I reflected as I passed through Hoxton. What was once a frightful slum full of street gangs and layabouts on the dole was now a delightful Yuppie estate. Most of the dinky Victorian terraces had been sandblasted and done up, with pristine E reg BMWs and Volkswagen GTis parked outside, glittering in the sunshine. Hoxton Street Market was selling skimpy designer tee shirts emblazoned with the motto SHARE THE WORLD, this season's fashion rage, for Kings Road prices, and the fruit stalls advertised kiwifruit, passionfruit, mangosteens and all the other hairy, puckered, impenetrable produce that was now so fashionable with the dinner party set. Aha, a thought struck me as I steered the Bentley through the well-heeled crowd. At last I knew how to get rid of those crates of dried-up South African oranges I'd been storing in a disused Cash 'n Carry in Wolverhampton for the past six months. Call them bossappies, call them bikofruit, whatever. An orange by any other name would taste twice as sweet to this lot. And cost twice as much, too, of course.

Hoxton was my kind of town. Haggerston was a different story altogether. The street Norman had directed me to was chockablock with rusty Allegros, dented Maxis and other tacky vehicles. I parked outside a derelict warehouse which sported an estate agent's board proclaiming with artful imagination 'HAGGERSTON HEIGHTS. 250 SUPERB HIGH SECURITY APARTMENTS FOR COMPLETION 1990. STUDIOS FROM £115,000'. I locked the car and, wishing the badge to my Bentley the long and happy life it was sure to receive in the possession of some beastly Beastie Boy fan, I searched my pockets for twenty pence pieces for the parking meter.

Damn it, I had no change and there wasn't anyone around who might change a bill except perhaps the busker playing his harmonica across the street. I walked over to him, holding out a £1 coin.

'Have you got ten pence for a cup of tea, Guv?' the blind busker asked as I approached.

'Yes, thanks,' I said as I put the pound back in my pocket and helped myself to a handful of change from the hat he'd set on the pavement before him.

'Thank you, sir. God bless you, sir,' the man replied as I jingled the coins that remained in the hat and replaced it on the ground.

'Not at all,' I assured him and nipped back across the street to feed the meter.

I found the building site just where Norman said it would be, but I couldn't locate any entrance. I squeezed between a couple of lose boards, cursing Norman as my trousers snagged on a rusty nail.

Opening what looked like the shed door Norman had described, I took out my torch and beamed it down the stone staircase of a long defunct tube station. I proceeded cautiously down the steps, avoiding as many cobwebs and strings of dust as I could. Norman was going to have to pay one hell of a hefty dry cleaner's bill for this one, I growled, as the stairs became a little more visible from the flickering light emanating from the platform. I clattered down the last few stairs with a thunderous echo.

'Norman!' I shouted into the Stygian gloom. I shuddered, imagining the likes of Boris Karloff and Bela Lugosi lurking in the shadows.

'Over here,' Norman's voice resounded eerily. I followed its direction and hurtled right off the platform on to the debris and metal-strewn tracks below. I lay stunned for a second, then felt myself for broken bones. Fortunately, everything but my suit was still intact. Norman leaned over the platform edge and helped me clamber out to the other side of the tracks. He brushed his hands daintily on the seat of his trousers.

'This had better be important, Norman,' I shouted. 'I've just ruined an eight hundred quid suit!'

'It doesn't matter. We'll soon both be wearing government-issue suits with big arrows over them!' Norman balled his well-manicured hands into fists and simply rounded on me. He hurled me against the wall of the platform, nearly knocking me out on the sharp edge of a chocolate machine. He certainly packed a lot of power, for a girl.

'You're touching me, Norman,' I said sweetly, trying to calm him and get him to loosen his grip on my already mangled lapels. 'Just tell me what's wrong.'

Norman released me. 'Hull Corporation are redeveloping Pilchard Street,' he announced in an ominous tone.

I shrugged. 'Means nothing to me.'

'Of course not. Now pay attention to me,' Norman instructed me as a train in the adjacent tunnel clattered by loudly. All I could make out in the din were the words, 'Plutonium oxide . . . deadly poison . . . Life Imprisonment. . . .'

'Say again,' I said as the noise subsided.

'You own a lock-up garage in Pilchard Street. Hull Corporation wishes to compulsorily purchase and demolish it,' he said through gritted teeth and waved an official-looking notice at me.

'So we'll sell,' I said nonchalantly, trying the wooden drawers on the chocolate machine. 'It's a lock-up garage. It's not a family heirloom.' I spied an old iron coupling on a pile of scrap on the platform near by. I picked it up, smashed the glass panel of the machine and removed a bar of Cadbury's Milk Chocolate.

'You've forgotten, haven't you?' Norman accused me in a dark tone.

'Forgotten what?' I asked guardedly, biting into the chocolate.

As I spat it out quickly on to the track, Norman reminded me, 'In 1982, General Galtieri paid you fifty-five thousand pounds to dispose of one thousand gallons of radioactive waste, didn't he?'

'Oh, that! That was before the Falklands business, Norman, so I hope you aren't impugning my patriotism?' I asked, staring stonily at the "Careless talk loses lives" poster on the opposite wall.

'Of course not, Alan, your patriotism is the finest money can buy!' Norman placated me with feminine guile. 'But the point is,' he got to the point. 'Where did we disposed of the waste?'

I began to see why he was so agitated. 'Pilchard Street?' I asked rhetorically.

'Exactly!' Norman confirmed and whimpered softly, 'What are we going to do?'

'Move it, of course,' I replied, attempting to appear calm, but my heart was beginning to thump with dread.

'But where to?' Norman asked sharply.

'We'll find another lock-up garage in another run-down Labour controlled inner city. There's plenty of them!' I exclaimed, suddenly remembering the soon-to-be-vacated Wolverhampton Cash 'n Carry.

I was about to share this solution with Norman when he shouted, 'But what if something went wrong? We're talking about deadly poison! I wouldn't be able to live with myself! I'd rather tell the authorities and take my punishment like a man.'

'But you're not a man any more, are you? Not a whole man,' I accused him truthfully. 'The Norman Bormann of 1982 was all for the Argentinian deal. But ever since you started the hormone treatment, you've been growing soft and sentimental.'

'Yes, I admit it. I'm proud to admit it!' Norman stated in a quavering voice. 'I'm becoming a woman. I'm growing more sensitive. Yes, it's true! Now what about the nuking waste?' He gulped and erupted into a flood of tears.

'I'll think of something,' I said, taken back by Norman's display of emotion, I handed him my handkerchief, pleading, 'For God's sake. Don't cry, please! I can't bear to see a grown trans-sexual cry. It's just too disgusting.'

I raced out of the underground and back into the sunlight.

I had to drive up to Haltemprice covered in grime and in my ragged suit as all my week-end gear is kept up there anyway and I would have caused a real sensation if I'd stopped off for a wash in a public loo on the way. I itched from all the grit, which was also ruining the Bentley's upholstery.

I arrived home shortly before seven and found Sarah in the dining room, laying the table for three.

'Alan, you're filthy,' she observed.

' "Am I? I'm surprised you can remember, it's been such a long time,' I replied lightly, alluding to our active sex life.

'I meant your suit. Where on earth have you been?' She sniffed.

'I had to visit a trans-sexual accountant in a disused railway station and I fell over the track,' I explained reasonably.

'If you have to lie to me, I wish you'd make more of an effort,' Sarah snorted, banging a platter of meat down on the table. 'She may have mauled you. I can see she didn't feed you.'

'All I've eaten is a disgusting square of pre-war chocolate,' I grabbed a slice of sausage from the platter, adding, 'I think I'll just have a shower.'

Don't be long, Daddy's here and he's staying for a bite to eat.'

That news really made my day. 'In that case I'll stay dirty or he'll think I made an effort,' I stated defiantly and poured myself a glass of wine.

Roland entered the dining room, holding an obviously empty glass aloft.

'Hello, Daddy' Sarah said brightly. 'Would you like a top up?'

'Is the Pope Polish?' he responded with his usual gruff charm and poured himself a few fingers of my scotch.

'This is a pleasant surprise, Roland,' I surreptitiously wiped my hand on the underside of the tablecloth and stretched it out to him.

He waved me away with, 'There's no need to lie, B'Stard. You're not in Parliament now.' He looked at me distastefully and observed, 'You look as if you've been down a coalmine!'

'No,' I retorted, quick as a whip. 'It's designer dust all the rage in London.'

'Is it?' Wouldn't put it past those metropolitan pansies,' Roland thumped his glass on the table.

'Shall we make a start,' Sarah broke our hostile silence and gestured to the table. We all sat down and unfurled our napkins.

'Charcuterie, Daddy?' Sarah offered Roland a platter of tasty-looking cold meats.

'What? Shark?' Roland barked, staring at the offending platter.

'No, charcuterie,' Sarah stressed with patience. 'Cold meats: it's a French word.'

Roland pushed the dish away from him. 'Oh, French! I should have guessed. You know I never touch anything French. Last time I touched something French was in 1940. Her name was Giselle and I was pissing glass for a month,' he brayed appreciatively at his own joke.

'And they say the art of dinner table conversation is dying out,' I remarked to the room in general.

'The ham's Danish, actually,' Sarah tried to tempt him with the meat again, but failed.

'Still European, though, isn't it. Factory farmed and saturated with hormones and phosphates. Two mouthfuls and you grow tits. If you ask me . . .'

'Nobody did,' I observed mildly, helping myself to some ham and a few slices of garlic sausage. I also heaped some potato salad onto my plate. There was very little left after Roland had taken his.

'. . . it's all an anti-British conspiracy by the Wops, Krauts and Dagoes in that unspeakable Common Market! And as for the French, words fail me. Unreliable crowd of swarthy little clap carriers,' Roland ranted on.

'Glass of Sancerre, then, Daddy,' Sarah said faintly.

Sir Roland picked up the bottle from the middle of the table and studied its label. 'French again, eh? Dare say it's fifty percent vinegar and fifty percent Jacque Cirac's brilliantine. Still, I'll give it a try,' he conceded gracelessly. He poured himself some, took a sip, and spat it back into the glass announcing, 'I was right.'

'It's always a delight when you drop in, Roland,' I said. 'Helps keep me in touch with what people are thinking, to use the word loosely, here in the constituency.' I tipped the remainder of the wine into my glass.

'If you ever showed your smug little face in this constituency, you'd know what people are thinking. They think their M.P.'s forgotten where Haltemprice is.'

'I was elected to serve – er' Sarah supplied 'Haltemprice.' 'Haltemprice, at Westminster, not to run the local Citizen's Advice Bureau.' I countered heatedly.

'You were elected because you're my son-in-law and I'm the Chairman of the local Conservative Party, and don't you forget it,' Roland thumped on the table, which, being wrought iron, caused him severe pain, I'm happy to report.

'Perhaps some cheese, Daddy?' Sarah offered desperately.

'Yes, do have some fromage,' I taunted him. 'There's Camembert, or Brie or Pont l'Eveque . . .'

'Or some fruit,' Sarah suggested quickly, reaching for the fruitbowl.

'Yes do have some French Golden Delicious,' I offered.

'Haven't you got anything South African?' He barked and chuckled to himself. If he but knew.

'I think I've got an Outspan Grapefruit in the fridge,' Sarah said quickly, springing to her feet. 'I'll get it,' she offered, making quickly for the kitchen.

'Now, to the purpose of my visit, Roland leaned back in his chair and levelled his gaze at me.

'Yes, enough of the social pleasantries,' I quipped.

'The annual village fête will be held next Sunday, in my grounds at Ingleborough Manor . . .'

I got out my filofax and flipped through it, prempting him with, 'It's rather short notice, Roland . . . but luckily I am free and . . .'

Roland looked at me in astonishment and said, 'You don't think I want you to open the fête?'

'Naturally,' I replied, hurt. 'I am the Member of Parliament . . .'

'And you'd milk the occasion for tawdry personal political

profit, Roland Magill has agreed to do the honours,' he elucidated as Sarah returned to the room with a peeled grapefruit on a laden tea tray.

'What, the dirty postcard fellow?' I shook my head in confusion.

'No, Roland Magill's from "Emmerdale Farm"! He's wonderful!' Sarah paused in her pouring of the tea and put her hand on her breast.

'You're asking some rustic to open the fête instead of me?' I asked incredulously.

' "Emmerdale Farm" 's a television programme, Alan, Roland Magill plays Amos Brearly,' Sarah illuminated me patiently. 'How jolly exciting, Daddy!'

'Thank you for the vote of confidence, dear wife . . .' I said sourly, 'I'll remember next time you want to go to London and rape Harrods.'

'Now, Sarah,' Roland directed, retrieving a memo pad and a pen from his jacket pocket. 'I'm putting you in charge of the victuals. Overseeing the local women, making sure there's plenty of wholesome English food, none of those damned quishes.' He turned his attention to me. 'And you, B'Stard, can donate the beer. We'll need two hogsheads of best bitter, one hogshead of mild and a firkin of scrumpy for the Morris dancers,' he ordered, ticking off his list.

'I'm sorry, "hogsheads". What's that in litres?' I asked to annoy him.

' "Litres"! "Litres"! This is Great Britain, B'Stard, not some poxy European enclave!' He shouted, absolutely apoplectic with rage. 'A hoghead's fifty-two and a half imperial gallons, emphasis on the word 'imperial"!'

I did a few sums on my calculator. Then I did them again. 'You're asking me to lay out nearly five hundred imperial pounds?'

'You can afford it,' Roland slapped my knee. '*Nouveau riche* little parvenu like you . . .'

'You don't mind using French words when they suit you, do you?' I batted his hand away and stormed from the room.

I could hear Roland saying to Sarah, 'French words. I didn't know that! buggered if I'll use them again,' as I went upstairs to wash and change before seeking refuge at my favourite pub.

I was at the Hangman's Knot Inn within half an hour, badly in need of liquid respite from my dear pa-in-law. The Public wasn't very crowded, with only a couple of regulars standing at the bar listening to Sidney regale them with tales from his golden past as he wiped glasses.

'Now that one,' Sidney was gesturing with his tea towel to one of the photos across the room, 'He was a bit simple-minded. I don't think the lad knew what was happening to him until I slipped the hood over his head, whereupon he pissed himself . . .'

'What, he was laughing?' A yokel asked in astonishment.

'No, I mean he had a little accident, Sidney winked at me in greeting as I came up to join the group. 'But it was a good clean hanging for all that.' Then, a week after I'd topped him, some other fellow confesses to the murder.' He laughed at the recollection, and philosophised, 'Still that's how it goes; can't make an omelette without breaking necks.' He concluded his tale and his audience sat down at their usual table and got out their dominoes.

'Hello, Sir,' Sidney addressed me. 'I was just reminiscing about the good old days.'

'I don't suppose you'd consider topping my father-in-law, just to keep your hand in? Cash job?' I asked, only half joking.

Sidney crooned soothingly, 'Old Gidleigh-Park's always been a cantankerous old bugger. Don't want to worry about him. . . .'

'And if he was dead I wouldn't,' I said, warming to the theme. 'Though hanging's too good for him! How about having him torn limb from limb between two teams of dray horses? Good publicity for the brewery.'

Sidney chuckled approvingly, 'Very imaginative, sir. I can see you'd have loved it in the olden days, when hanging was reserved for minor misdemeanours. Hardened criminals, they were hung, drawn and quartered.' He leaned over the bar and expanded, grinning broadly. 'That means they used to hang 'em, cut them down while they were still kicking, draw their entrails out of them with hooks, cut their bodies into four pieces, and stick their heads on a pole as a deterrent. All in public, of course.'

'Must have made a nice day out for the whole family,' I murmured, feeling a bit faint.

'If you want tea, by the way, the special's stuffed heart.' He licked his lips. I felt decidely queasy.

'No, I'll just have a large brandy.' Sidney poured one for me. I took it out of his hand and gulped at it eagerly. 'Changing the subject,' I sputtered, 'that old brewhouse behind the pub. Do you still use it?'

Sidney shook his head, replying, 'No, hasn't been used for brewing since before the war. I used to practice in it, mind, had my own little scaffold rigged up, but I haven't set foot in there since abolition. Why?'

'Well, in complete confidence,' I lowered my voice and cupped my hand round my mouth. 'I'm looking on behalf of . . . let's say a certain Department of State not unconnected with the Defence of the Realm, for some discreet storage space.'

Sidney clicked his tongue and shook his head sorrowfully. 'If only you'd asked me last Wednesday, sir.'

'Why?' I took another sip of my brandy.

'Because Thursday morning, this young property developer from Harrogate and her fiancé offered me £10,000 for it.

They're turning it into three duplex apartments, whatever they are,' he explained as he turned to serve a crusty-looking local with half a mild. I went to sit down at my favourite table, but the man tapped me on the shoulder, saying. ' 'Scuse me, but aren't you Alan Bastard, our Member of Parliament?'

'Please, when Mr B'Stard's here he's off duty,' Sidney reproved him in loyalty to my regular and lucrative custom.

'Far as I can tell, he's allus off bloody duty!' the unpleasant old git said, rapping his hand loudly on the bar. ' 'T'other night my little grandson asked me what "mythological" meant, and I told him it meant a fabulous non-existent creature, like a unicorn or our MP.'

'If you don't want banning, Vernon Heginbotham, you'll button your lip!' It was Sidney's turn to rap the bar.

'I don't care,' Vernon said with a defiant toss of the head. He drained his half pint and set the glass loudly on the bar. 'It'll be worth it for the chance to have me say at this elusive customer,' he continued, poking me in the chest with his knobbly finger.

'I'm terribly sorry, Mr B., shall I eject him?' Sidney offered, rubbing his hands together in preparation.

'No, no, let's hear him out, then throw him out,' I held Sidney in check and turned to face Vernon. 'All right, you oderiferous little prole you've got one minute.'

'What have you ever done for this constituency, you or your party?' Vernon began.

'What have we done? People have never been so well off! All my friends own BMWs and are making a fortune. There are more exclusive shops up here than there are in Knightsbridge!' I exaggerated only slightly and concluded, 'And you can't move for tourists in the summer.'

'But what about proper industry? Proper jobs? I remember when Britain was the workshop of the world,' Vernon's voice trembled. 'But you heartless new money-making Tories don't give a tinker's cuss for manufacturing!'

'Utter rot!' I objected hotly. 'I buy British! I drive a Bentley, my suits, shoes and shirts are all hand-made by British craftsmen, albeit with Greek surnames . . . .'

Vernon really lost his rag and shouted, 'I'm not talking of the poncy London carriage trade! I'm talking about proper jobs for us ordinary folk. Jobs for men, to use their hands, their muscles, their sweat,' he quavered.

'That's not a job, it's a gymnasium,' I replied with the contempt his sentimental little speech deserved.

'You may mock honest toil,' Vernon retorted. 'But I remember when we had the most profitable coalmine in the whole of Yorkshire!'

This was interesting. 'Coalmining? Here?'

'Ay, but you wouldn't know about that, you Tory toe rag!' Vernon sneered and shook his fist at me. Bored with his insolence, I kneed him in the groin and he slipped, groaning, to the floor under the bar.

'Why didn't I know about this coalmine?' I asked Sidney.

He shrugged, 'It closed after the General Strike in 1926. No one knows to this very day why it never reopened.'

'So let's get this straight,' I leaned on the bar and asked slowly, 'There's a large unused hole somewhere near here?'

'So they say, Sir,' Sidney confirmed with a nod.

'Where?' I narrowed my eyes.

'Don't ask me, Sir. Before my time.' Sidney breathed on a glass and polished it with his towel.

'Then who would know?' I persisted, patiently.

'The owner, of course,' he replied, setting the polished glass on the shelf behind him.

'The General Strike was in 1926!' I exclaimed despairingly. 'Is the owner still alive?'

Sidney chuckled, 'Yes, but he wouldn't be if you had your way, Sir. It's your father-in-law!'

Treating Sidney to a pint, I drained my brandy and quickly left the pub.

Luckily, Roland and Sarah were still at the table drinking tea when I arrived home, fired with determination to charm the whereabouts of the coal mine out of the old bastard.

My Georgian tantalus was on the table in front of Roland. It held three bottles of my best Scotch, port and brandy. And it was locked, Roland glared at it and at me balefully. I quickly took the key to the tantalus from my waistcoat pocket and unlocked it, remarking pleasantly, 'You look like a man who could do justice to a single malt.'

'Make that a double single malt,' Roland grunted, pressing his luck.

I went to the drawing room for tumblers, gritting my teeth into a fixed smile. Ordinarily the greedy bugger would be lucky to get a small single of Old Grouse out of me, but right now I had to pretend to be generous.

'So what have you two been talking about?' I inquired in an interested tone. As if I cared. I poured out two enormous glasses of malt whisky, passed my father-in-law the fuller of the two and joined my happy little family at the table.

'Daddy thinks it's high time we started a family,' Sarah said drily. How, I conjectured to myself? Immaculate Conception?

'Right you are, Father-in-Law, we'll get down to it the moment you go.' I raised my glass to him, toasting 'Here's mud in your eye' with all the smarm I could muster.

'You're after something, aren't you, B'Stard?' he asked suspiciously. I suppose I had laid it on a bit too thickly.

'No, just trying to be pleasant: make up for my execrable behaviour in storming out.' I laughed disarmingly and encouraged him to drink his malt. 'Darling,' I said to Sarah, 'I've bought you a present. It's out in the garden.' 'Really?' Sarah exclaimed, incredulously and trotted eagerly out of the French windows.

'So, Roland – Daddy.' I'd never called him that before and his reaction showed it was a mistake, 'good Scotch,' I grinned at him ingratiatingly.

'Yes, not bad,' Roland judged reluctantly.

I held up my tumbler and admired its pale amber contents. 'Twenty-five-year-old Glenoddle. They only make a couple of thousand cases every sixth year, so really, at fifty-three pounds a bottle, it's a snip.' I ostentatiously tipped another generous slug into Roland's tumbler.

Roland declared in a slightly more mellow tone, 'Then I was right. You have to be a *nouveau riche* little *parvenu* to afford the stuff.' He barked a short laugh and explained, 'Just my little joke.'

'Microscopic,' I whispered, temporarily forgetting myself. I switched the bonhomie back on and smiled, 'Now, about the beer for the fête; it'll be an honour to supply it. I've also been mulling over your criticisms for my political profile, and I realise you're right. I have been spending too much time at Westminster to the detriment of my constituency responsibilities.' What it cost me to make that speech had definitely got to be worth it.

'You know, B'Stard, perhaps you're not quite the unmitigated worm I've always thought you. . . .' Roland slurred gratifyingly and helped himself to more of my malt whisky.

'So,' I interrupted before he became too sloshed to spill the beans. 'Wearing my constituency hat, I'd like to ask you why Ingleborough Colliery didn't reopen after the General Strike?'

'Ingleborough Colliery?' Roland snapped, visibly taken aback.

'Don't you remember? Apparently you own it,' I remarked mildly.

'Oh, the colliery! It was over sixty years ago, the General Strike.' Roland's voice was now wary, as well as slurred.

'Go on,' I encouraged him.

'I was only twenty-one. My father had recently died, and the workforce was riddled with Communists. So, as the young new master, I had to make contingency plans to deal with the threat of revolution. . . .'

'Of course, of course,' I said sympathetically, adding, 'But that doesn't explain why you didn't reopen after the strike was crushed.'

'It was a long dispute, you see,' Roland paused to have another tipple of malt. 'And unfortunately, mine workings deteriorate rapidly when they aren't maintained. So, by the time we'd starved the men back to work, there wasn't any work for them to shuffle back to.' He shrugged at the historic inevitably of it all.

'How funny,' I said, genuinely amused. 'But just as a matter of local historical interest,' I inquired with supreme nonchalance, 'where was your mine, actually?'

Roland stiffened and said cagily, 'Hereabouts. . . .'

'Whereabouts exactly?' I persisted, offering him more Scotch.

Roland put his hand over his glass. 'Why don't you concentrate on Westminster and stop poking your nose into local affairs?' He growled and unaccountably stood up, grabbed his walking stick and stormed out into the night.

'I can't find my present.' Sarah came back into the room, shaking her head in confusion.

'There isn't one.' I laughed at her expression. 'It was a joke. Ha ha.'

'Peasant!' she hissed.

Then we heard the familiar noise of Roland's ancient Austin Cambridge backfiring, Sarah moaned, 'Oh no. He's brought the car! And he's drunk half a pint of whisky.'

'Sometimes, darling, you know just what to say to cheer me up,' I replied, biting thoughtfully into a French Golden Delicious. I poured myself another Scotch and locked the tantalus.

No one else in the area knew where the old mine was however

many drinks I bought for all the old codgers. If Norman and his miracle computer couldn't locate the mine, then I'd have to find another unused building to dump the waste. SDP Headquarters, perhaps?

Monday morning I went to meet Norman at his office, dressed for action in a pair of overalls I'd had the foresight to purchase on Saturday. I found him on the platform, studying an ancient torn and yellowing Ordnance Survey map, kitted out in similar attire to mine, which emphasised his new developments rather startlingly.

'Norman, you're looking quite curvaceous!' I greeted him jovially.

'Thank you, darling,' Norman said in a Fenella Fielding voice and pouted at me.

'And you can cut that right out!' I shouted, taken aback.

'I hope to, in due course. And when I'm a woman the authorities won't be able to touch me . . . unless they ask me nicely,' he preened, and then pointed to the map, declaring in his normal tone, 'This map dates back to 1921. The mine's clearly marked. You can see the entrance here,' he showed me, and continued, 'It's quite isolated. I've checked the 1982 map, and there doesn't seem to be any building above the mine.'

'Perfect.' I rubbed my hands together.

'Of course,' Norman went on, 'We should contact the county council to see if there have been any developments since 1982. . . .'

'Oh what a good idea. Then we could issue a press release saying Alan B'Stard's about to dump a thousand gallons of radioactive slurry in an area of designated natural beauty!' I clapped him on the back.

'Sorry, darling,' Norman simpered.

'Come on,' I said, collecting up the maps and hauling him to his feet. I began to propel him up the stairs.

'Get off,' Norman said in a shrill voice and shrugged off my hand.

Barring the occasional major slip-up, Norman's organisational skills are outstanding. He'd hired a transit van and all the gear we might need to transfer the tanker's contents to Sir Roland's abandoned mine.

We sped up to Hull and arrived in Pilchard Street in less than five hours. We parked half-way down the street from the lock-up and donned our radiation overalls and hoods in the back of the van. I picked up the geiger counter and Norman toted a heavy carry-all. Silently, we slid out of the van's back door and looked round.

Fortunately the street was deserted, except for a few snotty-nosed kids charging about and zapping each other with toy spaceguns. The kids scattered and ran for their lives when they saw what looked like two bono fide aliens.

I unlocked the garage's two high-security padlocks and we entered the dark lock-up. Norman pulled the cord on the overhead light. The geiger counter began to screech as we approached the tanker.

Working quickly and in silence, I held the stencil as Norman spray-painted both sides of the tanker with the words, 'Barker's Best Bitter'.

We wasted a little time and quite a bit of cover as we had to charge the tanker's battery with jump leads from the van, but as Pilchard Street was mercifully empty, it wasn't a real disaster, and the drive to Ingleborough proved a doddle.

We parked in a passing space on the country lane that the 1921 map indicated was nearest to the mine's approach. We removed our radiation suits and leaped down from the tanker's high cab, Norman clutching the 1982 map. Eventually we located the overgrown track, which we struggled along until we hit the almost invisible entrance to Ingleborough Colliery a few hundred yards later. It was set into the side of a hill, and almost entirely hidden by brambles and bushes. Its old iron gates were topped with loops of rusty barbed wire and sealed with heavy chains and dozens of padlocks.

'We're going to need some serious bolt cutters tonight . . . or perhaps a small tactical nuclear missle,' I announced, and Norman looked aghast. 'Joke, Norman. Come on,' and we retraced our steps to the tanker.

Suddenly we heard loud shouts and peels of childish laughter, coming from around a bend in the road. Crouching, we crept to investigate the noise and discovered a sign proclaiming

'HALTEMPRICE BOROUGH COUNCIL
INGLEBOROUGH JUNIOR SCHOOL'

Children were straggling out of the school gates, swinging satchels and fooling about.

'We can't dump it here!' Norman groaned softly.

'Why not?' I whispered.

'Because they've built a school above the mine, that's why not! You can't dump nuclear waste under an infants' school!' he proclaimed in a choked-up voice.

I didn't see what the problem was. 'It's only a council school. Their parents probably all vote Labour.'

'Politics don't come into it! They're children!' Norman burst into tears and tore off back up the road.

'Look, you old woman,' I panted, chasing after him. 'I'm sick and tired of your "Ban the Bomb" fellow-travelling appeasement.' I shook him by the shoulders to try and knock some sense back into him. 'If the British people have just voted for a British independent nuclear deterrent, so the British people should be proud to bear the tiny risk of having British nuclear waste under its schools,' I explained reasonably.

'But this is Argentinian nuclear waste!' the silly wimp continued to protest.

'That probably makes it less radioactive,' I assured him. 'They're not as efficient as we are.'

Norman shrugged me off and began to walk away, sniffing,

'I'm sorry, Alan, but I draw the line. You're on your own.'

'You walk out on me now, and you can whistle for the money for your sex change,' I threatened.

'I don't suppose I need your money any more!' Norman shouted, stamping his foot. 'The gamma rays coming off that truck, I wouldn't be at all surprised if I change species, let alone gender.' He minced defiantly down the road, away from the tanker.

Norman had really left me in the slurry. I desperately needed another pair of hands to accomplish the transfer, and after a little hard thinking later on the back lanes of Haltemprice, I came up with exactly whose strong hands it must be. Knowing his penchants, it took me but another moment to invent a suitably seductive line that would assure his complicity.

It was four o'clock and the Hangman's Knot Inn's carpark was empty when I arrived. I quickly took off my radiation gear, left it in the cab and hammered on the pub door.

'I wouldn't mind if I wasn't paying the girl by the hour,' I heard Sidney complaining as he shot the bolts. He opened the door to me, saying 'Oh hello, sir,' in a puzzled fashion as he struggled with the knot on his tie.

'Come in, come in,' he beckoned as I walked past him. 'I can't sell you a drink of course, or else I'd be in hot water with the licensing magistrates. But of course you'd know that, being one of them. . . .' he gabbled nervously.

'Stop gibbering, Sidney', I ordered him. 'I know you spend every afternoon in the company of Gina, busty Eurasian masseuse. It's nothing to be ashamed of,' I winked and slapped him heartily on the back.

'Isn't it?' Sidney looked at me for reassurance.

'Of course not,' I complied. 'The girl is self-employed; she's doing her bit for Britain instead of lying about in bed all day. . . .'

'She does lie in bed all day,' Sidney corrected me.

'Yes,' I agreed. 'But it's not her bed,' I qualified as I led Sidney to the privacy of the Snug.

'Now, I'm going to confide in you, Sidney,' I lowered my voice and announced portentously.

'Are you, sir? Thank you, sir. . . .'

'This is in the strictest confidence. Really no one should know who hasn't signed the Official Secrets Act. . . .'

Sidney clapped his hand over his heart and interrupted, 'But I have signed it, sir. All us Official Executioners had to,' he swore.

'Good,' I nodded importantly. 'Then I can tell you that the PM has decided that the next vote on capital punishment will not be a free vote.' I touched the side of my nose confidentially.

'That's wonderful, sir. Fantastic news . . . what does it mean, actually? Sidney asked excitedly.

'It means that this time next year, the prison population will start to drop sharply . . . if you catch my drift.' I demonstrated by yanking his tie upwards.

Sidney did catch my drift. 'You mean I'll get my old job back, sir? he gurgled.

I yanked his tie harder, and inquired, 'Who do you think is going to be Minister for Death?'

Sidney gasped. 'You, sir?' I nodded gravely and Sidney pumped my hand. 'Congratulations, sir!' He swallowed gratefully when I released his tie.

'So, stick with me, and it'll be money for old rope,' I laughed, then added, 'Now, there's one tiny service you can do me, Sidney. . . .'

I loaded the empty barrels from round the back of the pub into Sidney's car shortly after closing time. Sidney fancied driving the tanker, so I took his car and led the way to the mine, lurching precariously across the overgrown terrain.

We bashed at the rusty padlocks with rocks. They were surprisingly easy to break open. We parked as close as we could to the mine entrance and rolled the barrels to the tanker. Sidney hosed the lethal cocktail from the tanker into the barrels, which I plugged and inspected carefully by torchlight, having put the radiation suit on again.

We'd filled about twenty barrels in companionable silence when Sidney said, 'If you don't mind me asking, sir, why are we pumping beer into a disused coalmine? Unless it isn't beer. . . .'

'I can see you're not as stupid as you look, Sidney,' I complimented him as we continued working.

'Thank you, sir,' Sidney said with pride, panting slightly as he heaved one of the barrels to the mine entrance.

'So, let's just say that what I don't tell you, the Russians can't torture out of you,' I said, shining my torch in his eyes.

'Ah, get you, sir,' Sidney said, shielding his eyes with one arm.

When we finished filling the barrels I got the rope ladder from the cab of the tanker. I unfurled it and Sidney tied its ends professionally to the gateposts.

'Right, now here's what I want you to do.' I instructed him. 'Lower yourself into the mine. I'll roll the barrels down the slope. You catch them and do the necessary.' I pushed him toward the rope ladder.

Sidney resisted me and gulped, 'I'm sorry, sir, I can't go down that pit, even for you.'

'Why not?' I fumed.

'I'm afraid of depths, sir.' Sidney admitted in an embarrassed voice and looked at his feet.

'Afraid of what?' I couldn't believe my ears.

'Depths, sir,' Sidney repeated obediently. 'Some people are afraid of heights, I'm afraid of depths. That's why all the beer in my pub is in barrels above the counter, so's I don't have to go down into the cellar,' he explained.

Just what I needed. A useless hangman just hanging about doing nothing. 'You're mad, aren't you?' I stated the obvious.

'Well,' Sidney demurred. 'More neurotic than psychotic, sir. My psychotherapist says it's my unconscious guilt about preparing all those people for the long drop.'

'All right, all right,' I silenced his psychobabble. 'I'll do it myself! But I must warn you, when the Death Penalty Bill comes up for its third reading, I'm going to table an amendment in favour of the Electric Chair!' I positively enjoyed shouting this at him.

'That's not fair, sir,' Sidney whined at me, toeing the earth. 'I don't know my AC from my DC.'

That made two of them. Perhaps I should fix Sidney up with Norman, I thought, and ordered, 'Shut up and get the barrels. You're not afraid of barrels, are you, Sidney?'

I trained the powerful beam of my torch into the entrance of the mineshaft. I made my way down a gentle slope and almost immediately encountered a wall of what seemed to be oildrums, which completely blocked any further progress.

'What the . . .?' I exclaimed and read the red lettering on the drums aloud in astonishment, ' "Danger! Mustard Gas! Deadly Poison! Best before December 1927"!'

As a rat scurried over my foot, a familiar voice sounded out from behind me. 'As I was saying, I had to make contingency plans to deal with the threat of revolution.' Gidleigh-Park grinned wolfishly – I knew at once that lily-livered transexual Bormann had grassed on me, 'but for fifty-five thousand pounds . . . that's what the Argies paid you, isn't it . . . I'll show you my disused quarry.'

I turned to him, astonished. 'Roland Gidleigh-Park, you're a bigger bastard than I am!' I exclaimed, impressed.

'Yes,' he acknowledged shortly. 'Got ya.'

Yes, he had, the old bastard. *This time.*

CHAPTER FIVE

FRIENDS OF ST JAMES

I was driving along to school, still wondering if it had been Norman who'd informed on me re the £55,000 and the Argies. On balance, I had to accept his denials as he'd maintained his innocence even when I'd offered to complete his sex change for him on the spot, using my Swiss Army knife. I concluded Gidleight-Park had had my Bentley bugged and made a mental note to take it for a valet service cum security screening as soon as I got back to London.

It was my old school's annual Founder's Day Prize Giving and, I of course, I had been chosen to be guest speaker. I remembered these occasions at Fiskes so well. In my three years there I'd got the prize for Debating Skills each time and when I was in the Upper Sixth form they'd even instituted a new prize just for me: Junior Entrepreneur of the Year. I wondered whether Fiskes still presented that award as I parked the Bentley in the space that had been reserved for me. If so, I'd earmark some time for its recipient; Norman's defection to the distaff side was making me seriously consider our on-going relationship and I could use a fresh, young masculine ally whose reliability wasn't in question.

A Range Rover parked in the space next to me. A couple in their thirties got out as I was locking the car door. The man immediately recognised me and as he introduced me to himself and his overdressed wife, a young lad of about thirteen interrupted us boisterously.

'Hello, super of you to come!'

The man looked at him and replied brusquely, 'We had to, our son's a pupil here. Costs a fortune, but at least it keeps him out of our hair.'

His wife whispered, 'Roderick this is our son.'

The man peered closely at the boy and said, 'So it is! Roddy. How you've grown!'

Reflecting on why I had never invited my own parents to Prize Giving, I left the happy little family chatting in the carpark and made my way to the headmaster's study for the sherry reception which always preceded the speeches. Both the sherry and the company were bound to be unspeakable, but as Guest of Honour I had to do my bit.

The Head shook my hand warmly and barked some inane pleasantries at me. Handing me a glass of sherry, he led me to a small group of prosperous-looking businessmen.

'. . . and in five years I'd built my turnover up to thirty million per annum. . . .'

'Thirty million!' I repeated, impressed. 'Ever thought of having an MP on your letterhead? Good for the old corporate image,' I suggested, artfully.

The businessman looked me up and down and continued, 'Then I said to myself, "What's it all for? Is it making you happy?"'

'It would make *me* happy!' I replied.

'So I gave the company away to the workers and went to live in Nepal.'

'Gave it away to the workers? That's treason!' I exclaimed in shock.

'In Katmandu, I studied with the great Lama. . . .'

I abandoned that bunch of senile hippies and, taking a sip of sherry, looked around the room for someone to amuse me. The sherry was vile. I searched the room for a pot plant or something to pour the rest into and settled for the Head's upturned mortar board on the mantelpiece.

A West Indian person wearing an ornate but gaudy uniform covered in quite realistic medals clasped me over-intimately on the shoulder with his right hand, shouting, 'Alan, long time no see!'

'Do I know you?' I asked frostily, removing his hand from me.

'Lance Okum-Martin!' he introduced himself, beaming. 'I used to be your fag.

'Of course, little Lance!' I said, recollecting the lazy little bugger at once. 'So what's become of you since school? No, don't tell me, let me guess.' I sized him up. 'Doorman at the Empire, Leicester Square?' I flicked his epaulettes and revised, 'No, must be at least Senior Doorman, with all this braid! Well done, Lance! I'll look you up if I'm ever in the market for two front stalls.'

Lance interrupted my departure by placing a restraining hand on my arm. 'Actually, old boy, the uniform denotes that I'm President for Life of The Republic of St James,' he announced, to my immediate interest.

'Really? President for Life?' As we shook hands I added, 'Must, pay well . . .'

'It's only a very poor island, Alan,' he replied with becoming modesty. I didn't believe him, naturally.

Of course, of course, all you Third World countries are stony broke, but that doesn't seem to stop you Presidents for Life all running seventeen wives and a fleet of Mercedes,' I joked.

'Not me, old boy. One fiancée and a Sinclair C5,' Lance averred, looking at the carpet humbly.

'Pull the other leg, it's got a hand-made shoe on,' I laughed.

'Truly,' Lance assured me. 'We are poor because we don't have any banks, so it's very hard for our farmers to obtain finance for their unique tobacco exports.'

'Yes,' I said, suddenly bored to death. 'Well, it's been marvellous seeing you again. We must do this every twelve years.' I tried to give him the brush-off, but again he restrained me, pleading, 'Can't you help us, Alan, as a Member of Parliament, and for the sake of the school?' Ah yes, the school. The good old school.

'No,' I told him as I beckoned an ancient waiter. 'I say, I wonder if as Guest of Honour, I'm entitled to something better than Cypriot Amontillado?' The waiter deafly ignored me and tottered off. I wanted to put him in his place, but Lance was persistent in his pestering.

'But our St. James' tobacco is very special. At least try some,' he exhorted me, and slipped a long, loosely-rolled cheroot between the lips I had just opened to tell him to push off. Lance lit the cigar with a gold lighter and resigned I inhaled deeply. I took a few more puffs and the room suddenly blurred.

'Mellow, wouldn't you say?' Lance prompted me, replacing his cigarette case in his pocket.

'Yes, it's certainly . . .' I took another suck, at a loss for words. 'Certainly, certainly . . .' I rocked back on my heels. The room had started to go round and round and round . . .

Dimly I heard Lance wheedle, 'I don't suppose you could lend me a thousand pounds?' Lance asked urgently. 'Only coming from a country without any banks . . .'

And then I became vaguely aware of a well-manicured black hand removing my chequebook and helping me to fill it in.

A short while later, we all piled into the school hall for the speeches. I sat next to Lance on the stage with all the other old boys and the staff, happy as a sand boy. The Headmaster's introductory remarks were most amusing and I was still chortling as he began to introduce me.

'. . . So with no more ado, I call upon the Member for Parliament for Haltemprice, Yorkshire, Old Fiskean and future Prime Minister . . .'

I stood up, giggling, but managed to suppress it as the Head finished, 'Alan Beresford B'Stard.'

I walked unsteadily to the lectern, attempting to pull myself together.

'Thank you, Headmaster,' I said as I knocked his mortar board off. I got out my notes and put them on the lectern. This was one speech I'd have to read, as my mind had gone completely blank. As blank as pages on the lectern. 'Where have my notes gone?' I turned a page over. What a relief. 'Oh, they're written on the other side. Excellent. Okay . . . right. Now, why've I got the biggest majority in the House of Commons? Anyone? As no one from the blurry audience chose to respond, I went on, 'It's because more people voted for me than anyone else, of course! They all put their crosses in my box. Pathetic, the number of people who can't even write their names! That's why we need schools like this, to keep us apart from Them, to stop Them dragging us down. So don't talk to me about the education crisis. Look around this beautiful school. Nothing wrong with the education system that £2,500 a term can't put right, is there?'

I nodded at the audience, who all nodded back at me, as did the hall. I gripped the lectern and continued reading, 'Ditto the so-called housing shortage. There are thousands of empty houses if you know where to look. I mean, the Algarve is empty six months out of the year. Yes, what we need in this country are radical solutions, shooting straight from the hip, which brings us on to the Health Service.' Headmaster stood up clapping and smiling nervously.' Thank you, Alan,' he said, but I wasn't finished yet.

'We hear so much Lefty whingeing about the NHS waiting lists. After all, in the good old days, you got ill, and if you were poor, you died. Today everyone seems to think they have the right to be cured. Result of this sloppy socialist thinking? More poor people. In contrast, my policies would eliminate poor people, so eradicating poverty. And they say Conservatives have no heart. Thank you very much,' I concluded to a few seconds of complete silence and then a tumultuous standing ovation.

I honestly can't recall if anyone did win the Junior Entrepreneur of the Year award.

Norman's new office which was concealed within a desanctified church in Parsons Green. It was the afternoon of our regular weekly session to catch up on each others' news and generally shoot the breeze. I promised Norman I'd be there with some reluctance, as Annette, my skilful secretary, and I had arranged to tryst the night away, and Parsons Green is not on my regular route to Stringfellows.

I arrived at the church at five o'clock. Pushing the entryphone button, I gave our latest password, 'Edwina Currie detests fags.'

A deep voice emanated from the entryphone speaker, proclaiming, 'This is the Reverend DuBarry. Evensong is at six thirty. We have to keep the church locked up because of the vandals and the tourists.'

'Norman,' I sighed long-suffering, 'Norman, it's me, Alan. Let me in.'

The door opened with an electronic buzz and I entered the musty church.

Norman had set his desk up in the choir. He came up the aisle to greet me, tottering on pink high-heeled pumps, which looked just a wee bit out of keeping with his suit. I could see he'd been going to town on the make-up: violet eye shadow with matching mascara, blusher and pancake foundation. The whole works were somewhat spoiled, however, by his moustache.

'Sorry to be so jumpy,' Norman apologised, patting his hair. 'But the hormone treatment plays havoc with my nerves . . . and I'm sure a strange man was following me back from the hairdressers yesterday.'

'I'm not surprised,' I said. 'Have you looked in the mirror lately?'

'No, have you looked in *The Telegraph*?' he replied as we walked down the aisle together like bride and groom.

Norman handed me a copy of *The Telegraph* from his desk, saying, 'They liked your speech yesterday; there's a third leader talking about you as a future PM.'

I glanced at the paper he held out. 'Only page seven though,' I said, disappointed, adding, 'Do you mind if I take a pew?'

Norman gestured expansively round the church, 'Take them all. It's not my church.'

'Norman, what do you know about St James?' I asked, seating myself on a dusty pew.

Norman pressed some buttons on his computer keyboard.

'Do you mean St James the Great, son of the fisherman Zebedee; St James the Just, eldest of the brethren of Jesus or St James the Park, home of Newcastle United Football Club?' Norman culled an assortment of sanctified Jims from his prodigious memory banks.

'I mean the Caribbean island of St James,' I announced, stumping him for a moment.

'Doesn't ring any tills,' he admitted pressing some more keys. 'Ah, here it is. "St James, Caribbean island . . . thirty-seven square miles . . . Capital, St James City",' he read aloud.

'An original mind at work there,' I observed sardonically. I put my feet on my pew and stretched out as Norman continued.

' "population 9,200. President for Life, The Honourable L.F.K. Okum-Martin . . ." ' so Lance was telling the truth, I said to myself. 'What about it?' he asked.

'I met Okum-Martin a couple of days ago at my old school Founders' Day. Used to be my fag,' I explained from my supine position.

'They allowed black boys in your school?' Norman looked at me in mild surprise.

'Of course. It was a very liberal regime, as long as they could afford the fees and didn't mind being called velcro-head,' I said, flicking my hand. 'Anyway, I lent him £1,000 . . .'

'But presumably you made him put his island up for security,' Norman added for me eagerly. And wrongly.

'No, I didn't!' I banged my head on the seat of the pew. 'Actually, my memory of the whole day is rather hazy.'

'But why should the President of a sovereign nation state be short of the necessary?' Norman inquired as he switched off his computer.

'It's a very small island and they don't have any banks, apparently,' I enlightened him and yawned.

'No banks!' Norman exclaimed in an agitated fashion and began to pace the aisle. 'How very interesting.'

'Interesting?' I was rigid with boredom. 'Explain,' I commanded him. I couldn't see where this was going and anyway I'd already mentally kissed my thousand pounds good-bye.

'If there aren't any banks, then you ought to get him to let you start one. We could make millions!' His shrill voice resounded through the church.

I sat up, my juices flowing again. 'Millions? That's my favourite number. How?'

'We offer high interest rates, no taxation, no exchange controls and total confidentiality,' he enumerated with enthusiasm. 'Then when you've ensnared a sufficient number of avaricious cretins . . .'

'Prudent investors,' I cut in, already envisaging our sales brochure.

Norman continued, 'To deposit their ill-gotten gains . . .'

'Hard earned savings,' I amended.

'Well, then . . .' Norman paused dramatically for effect.

'Yes, yes!' I urged him to get on with it.

'The bank goes out of business and all the money disappears!' he announced, arms opened wide.

'Into my pocket!' As Norman nodded, I exclaimed, 'Brilliant! Let's do it.'

Norman frowned and placed his hands on his hips, suddenly deflated. 'Where are you going to find a large number of rather stupid and very greedy people with enough money to invest in a dubious get-rich-quick scheme like this?'

I assured him I knew just the place. 'Norman, where do I work?'

Due to my prolonged meeting with Norman, there had been no time to get Annette a little prezzie before I met her in the wine bar, so this morning I graciously offered her a generous tip instead. She told me where to stick my tip and stormed out of my flat. Typical bloody woman. I was now on the look-out for a new secretary, and meanwhile had to make-do. Consequently, I hadn't been able to do much more this working day than locate Lance Okum-Martin and invite him to meet me in the Stranger's Bar that same evening. First things first.

Then I had phoned Beatrice to invite her to dine at the House tomorrow evening, but she said that she had a previous engagement, unfortunately, 'With whom?' I asked, on my high horse, and she replied that Sarah was coming down to London for a couple of days' worth of shopping and was staying with her in her London flat. Apparently, Beatrice had persuaded her not to interrupt my difficult schedule and Sarah was going to camp out on Beatrice's sofa while skinning my Platinum American Express Card of at least ten layers of plastic and draining my liquid assets like Pimms No. 1 on a hot summer's day. I offered to take them both to dinner, but Beatrice assured me that Sarah would be too tired to face anything more than a scrambled egg and a night in front of the telly with her. I can't say I was too disappointed, as pulling Beatrice in front of my wife would be considered a bit crass in anybody's book.

I met Lance at the entrance to the Bar at the appointed hour. Instead of his military regalia he was wearing a sober grey suit, thank God.

We greeted one another with all the matiness of old school chums and I cleared a boring Labour henchman of Bob Crippen, Len Catchpole, and some *Morning Star* hack from the table I desired after only a handful of insults.

We sat down and ordered our drinks. Fortunately, the bar didn't stock overproof rum or lime, so Lance settled on a Cuba Libre and I ordered my usual double Armagnac.

'I suppose you're wondering why I invited you here tonight, Lance?' I asked as the waiter brought our drinks.

Lance leaned forward, a serious expression on his face. He said, 'Alan, if you're worried about your thousand pounds, I'm expecting an international letter of credit from the World Health Organisation for $50,000. It's supposed to be for a new clinic, but as I am also Minister of Health . . .'

'Don't worry about the money,' I scolded him jovially, raising my glass to him. 'Cheers!'

'Bottoms up,' Lance returned, looking relieved.

'As we used to say in the Fifth Form Remove,' I winked, then continued seriously. 'You see, I want you to consider the thousand pounds as an investment in your poor but worthy homeland.'

Lance raised an eyebrow at me over the rim of his glassful of rum 'n coke. 'What do you mean, exactly?'

'I've been worrying about the sorry plight of your struggling impoverished little farmers and I think I might be able to help,' I answered in the style of Sir Stephen Baxter. 'So, I'm prepared to set up a bank for you.'

At this moment the Division Bell chose to ring. Most of the occupants of the Bar drained their glasses and fled.

'What's that, the fire alarm?' Lance asked hastily.

'No, it's just the Division Bell,' I told him reassuringly.

'Some trivial vote about old age pensions or something. We've got a majority of a hundred and two; I'm sure they won't miss me,' I smiled and carried on. 'You'd like a bank, wouldn't you?'

'That's very considerate, but there's really no need. We're a simple people. . . .' Lance broke off and looked round the emptying room in confusion.

'No, no, no. It's the least I can do for an Old Fiskean.' I urged him to finish his drink and summoned the waiter to order another round. 'All I need is your go-ahead. . . .'

'Well,' Lance hesitated, obviously not wanting to appear to accept charity too readily. He remarked, 'Constitutionally speaking, I should consult the National Representative Council. . . .'

'Don't give me all those old coconuts, Lance,' I pooh-poohed the unnecessary parliamentary procedure. 'You're President for Life, don't go on pretending it's a democracy!' I opened my attaché case and withdrew the contracts Norman had drawn up and had biked to me himself that afternoon, saying, 'My advisors have drawn up the relevant documents. All we need is your signature on these papers.'

I passed the documents over to Lance, along with my fountain pen, which I uncapped for him. Lance glanced over the contracts for a couple of moments. 'If you're absolutely sure,' he said uncertainly, pen poised over the signature line. 'But I think there should be something rather more in it for me than your admittedly gracious grand,' he suggested.

'Of course,' I winked subtly at him over my Armagnac. 'And there is. As President for Life, we would be honoured to have you on our Board of Directors, and so you'd get the usual kickbacks.'

'That's only to be expected.' Lance considered his drink and removed its slice of lemon. 'But tell me, Alan, where do you propose to house this bank?' He nibbled thoughtfully on the lemon before continuing, 'After, all office accommodation is in very short supply on our tiny overcrowded island, and I own the only office building . . .'

'How much?' I asked smartly, reaching for my chequebook. I'm nobody's fool.

Most of the remainder of my week was taken up by assiduous attendance at all sessions, however tedious, assessing the mood of the House. I had to gauge precisely the correct moment to make my announcement for maximum impact in order to start my word-of-mouth publicity campaign for my stunningly original charity appeal.

On Thursday evening as midnight approached. I'd had about enough. An Adjournment Debate on foreign aid was in interminable progress. Even the Minister for Foreign Affairs was snoring loudly as the Shadow Minister for Foreign Affairs, emphasis on the word 'shadow', that useless Bolshevik cypher, Catchpole, droned on in his Brummy accent, '. . . I have the figures here: United Kingdom 0.47 percent, Federal Republic of Germany, 0.85 percent. . . .'

My personal cellnet phone rang just then, nearly startling the life, or what passed for it, out of my colleagues. I removed the phone from my pocket and answered it immediately, ostentatiously extending my aerial. 'Yes?' I whispered urgently, expecting the caller to be Norman with a new angle which might affect the tenor of my proposal to the House, but it was Trixi, an enticing new business contact whose marketing flair had caught my attention with a cunningly-worded self-advertisement slipped under the door of my London flat and whose professional development I was fostering in my own time.

'No,' I assured her, 'it shouldn't go on much longer . . . Because I'm about to speak! Yes, I've got the olive oil. Have you got the block and tackle? . . . Great! Now, just remind me, it's second left off Streatham High Road, isn't it?'

Having double-checked the directions, I hung up. Catchpole was still boring the Chamber with his meaningless statistics.

'... France, 0.66 percent; Luxembourg, 1.25 percent....'

I rose to my feet decisively. If the ducks weren't sitting now, they never would be. Besides, I had other pressing affairs to attend to. I'm a busy man and Catchpole was wasting my time.

'No,' the boring sod glared at me and said, 'I do not give way to the Honourable Member for Haltemprice. I've got lots more statistics to give the House....'

'The House doesn't want them!' I asserted loudly on behalf of my assembled colleagues, rousing at least half the attendant rabble from their slumbers. 'The House needs your statistics like it needs another Guy Fawkes!'

'... Italy, 0.75 percent; Holland, 0.89 percent; Denmark 0.77 percent....' Catchpole droned on more loudly.

I stamped my foot impatiently, saying, 'Oh, shut up! This is even more mind-numbing than the Eurovision Song Contest....'

'... France....' Catchpole continued, flustered.

'You said France!' I accused him of repetition. 'Sit down!'

'Order! Order!' the Speaker dictated in weary tones.

'If I said France twice, that's because it's a very important country,' Catchpole said in a futile attempt to be droll.

'Ha, ha, ha. That was meant to be a joke, wasn't it? Only I don't see Mr Deputy Speaker laughing.'

On hearing his job title mentioned, the Deputy Speaker opened his eyes like Alice's doormouse and squeaked, 'Order!'

Catchpole sat down, completely defeated as the House laughed in appreciation at my joke. I struck a parliamentary pose and began to orate, 'We have heard from the Honourable Member for Birmingham Stretchford, a depressingly dreary little constituency which he suits admirably, droning on about how we don't give enough foreign aid.'

Over Catchpole's protests, I continued, 'I say we give too

much, particularly to tinpot little dictators who aren't even decently grateful! If we must give our money away to foreigners, we should give it to pro-British tinpot dictators,' I started the gist of my spiel to automatic and somewhat somnolent cries of 'Hear, Hear!' from my lot and jeers of 'Rubbish!' from across the House.

'We should aid our allies, such as the loyal little nation of St James. This brave country, which offered its services to Great Britain during the Falklands conflict,' I admonished them, 'If you like the Falklands so much, then go and live there!' bawled some Labour hack.

'Oh, the Mogadon's worn off, has it?' I retorted and doggedly, carried on, 'The St Jamesians were willing, nay, eager, to be used as a strategic staging post. That they proved to be in the wrong ocean wasn't their fault, but a cruel trick of geography. And yet what aid do these fine people receive? Not a farthing! Yet here is a struggling little country that has not taken the Communist path; that indeed is so keen to encourage foreign investment that the Bank of St James pays twenty-five percent tax free interest on foreign deposits of over £10,000. That's right,' I paused and then reiterated more loudly, 'twenty-five per-cent tax free!'

This caused the excitement mayhem I had anticipated, and from both sides of the House. Unfortunately, my phone rang again at that precise second. It was Trixi. I hissed 'Not now!' into the mouthpiece and rang off rapidly to continue milking the crowd.

Even dim old Catchpole was hooked by the percentage rate I had announced. 'Twenty-five percent tax free! Any likelihood of them opening a branch in my constituency?' He stood up and asked in a friendly way.

'Even the trees don't have branches in your constituency!' I declared.

Thus skilfully putting him down, I strode from the Chamber

to appreciative laughter on both sides of the House.

Having effectively accomplished the first stage of my mission, sowing the seeds of greed necessary to my St James venture, I judged it time to sow some of my own very wild oats.

Horniman Press printed up the glossy brochures for the 'Parliamentary Friends of St James' in record time. The three hundred embossed, foiled folders were more expensive than the entire printing of *Sex is Wrong* had been, but the potential return on my initial investment was going to make the expense insignificant.

Piers and I slipped a complimentary St James cheroot into every folder and handed out the package to each Member as he entered the Committee Room I'd reserved for the function. Soon sounds of genial laughter and wafts of pungent smoke permeated the corridor, beckoning a couple of dozen more back and front benchers of all complexions. Within minutes I had to stick a 'House Full' sign on the door.

I started the ball rolling with a sing-along rendition of the St James National Anthem, a sentimental little marching ditty I'd composed myself the day before. My audience joined in merrily, waving their 'cigars' in the air to the beat.

I then went on to extol the virtues of St James and its unique banking system, concluding my opening pep talk with an allusion to St James' export potential, the stunningly mellow blend of tobacco they were almost all enjoying.

'. . . and I'm sure you'll all agree that this marvellous tobacco deserves the financial backing to compete on the international market.'

I noticed Catchpole giggling helplessly at the back of the room.

'The Shadow Spokesman for Foreign Affairs can either stop his childish giggling or go to stand in the corridor,' I admonished him, before things got too out of hand.

'I'm sorry, I just can't help it,' Catchpole spluttered, setting off his entire row into gales of laughter.

I paused as they wiped their eyes and generally succeeded in collecting themselves. A Labour Member in the third row raised his unlit cheroot at me.

'Mr Chairman, are you absolutely sure this is tobacco?' he asked, sniffing the air accusingly.

'This is the real world, Fiddick. Nothing is sure! Go and live in Albania if it's certainty you want.'

As Fiddick sat down, squashed, I continued, 'Now, with the Parliamentary Recess approaching, I propose that we, The Friends of St James, fly out to this beleaguered little island to study its problems at first hand.'

I winked at Piers in the front row, who, after a few seconds, realised my cue and stood up.

'I second the proposal. It is the patriotic duty of all of us to support this ally and invest in their future, at twenty-five percent tax free per annum,' he recited parrot fashion to choruses of 'hear, hears'.

'Thank you, Mr Fletcher-Dervish. Just the sort of chap this organisation needs as Secretary. All in favour?' I asked, to an automatic erection of hands.

'Hold on, you only asked me to. . . .' Piers said, frowning. I drowned out his protest with, 'Unanimous, excellent! Piers Fletcher-Dervish, come on down!' said in my best Leslie Crowther imitation. The audience whooped and cheered automatically as Piers reluctantly joined me on the platform.

'Now, who's in for a fact-finding mission to the sunny Caribbean where the azure sea laps a golden beach, and the dusky maidens lap the visiting parliamentarians?' I beckoned them forward with a wave and they all stampeded to the platform, jostling to join the queue.

'The Friends of St James honours all major gold credit cards,' I told the queue thoughtfully as I withdrew a miniturised credit card machine from my attaché case.

Forty-two Parliamentary Friends of St James eventually crammed themselves into the ancient piston-engined Dakota I'd hired to take us on the last lap of our journey from Miami to St James Island. Hiring a jet for the hour's flight had seemed a waste of money, but maybe my policy of 'every expense spared' was going to be slightly revised in future, that is, if I survived the jaunt in this clapped-out crate.

Piers and I grabbed the only seats with any leg-room, fastened our seatbelts and watched our hostess, Cyndy, who looked just like a Barbie Doll, go through the usual song and dance about emergency exits and flotation vest with more than usual attention. I wouldn't mind sliding down a blow-up chute with that little corker between my legs.

The entire plane juddered as we struggled to lift off. After a number of breathless minutes lurching about in the sky, the 'No Smoking' sign went off and our pilot's bland American voice sounded over the intercom, garbled by the blaring and blatting of the plane's propellers.

'Well, sorry about the technical hitch, folks. No one's ever gotten any chewing gum when you need it. Still, we finally plugged the leak and we're airborne,' he said cheerily, as we all looked at each other in alarm. The voice continued, 'My name is Bobby J. Hirsch III and I'm your Captain. The flying time to Hanoi . . . what? sorry, St James is approximately one hour. God bless you for flying Caribbean International Airways. God Bless Mom and Dad, and God help President Reagan,' Cap'n Bob finished.

Cyndy passed us round after round of free alcohol, which we all eagerly tossed down our throats to calm our nerves.

Forty-five minutes of hazy drunkenness later, Pier pressed the recline button on the arm of his seat. The seat collapsed backwards on to Catchpole, who emitted an angry, muffled squawk. Piers struggled out of his seatbelt and went to revive Catchpole with profuse apology. He returned to his seat, put it in an upright position, and sat down with a sigh, sweaty and dishevelled. Wiping his brow with his silk handkerchief, he sighed, 'What an awful journey. I'm really knackered.'

Catchpole stood up drunkenly and leaned over the back of my seat.

'Bit cramped, this plane, isn't it, Bastard,' he complained loudly.

'My words exactly,' I nodded up at him. 'I should never have let Piers make the travelling arrangements.'

'I didn't!' Piers protested weakly as Catchpole glared at him.

'You get more luxury on Aeroflot,' Catchpole muttered.

'Hear that, Piers?' I slapped him on the knee, claiming. 'You're my witness. Labour Front Bench Spokesman admits he's a Communist! Wait until the papers hear about that!'

Catchpole blinked and shook his head. 'Excuse me, must have a tinkle,' he said vaguely and started fumbling with an Emergency Exit door just across the aisle.

'Why did you charter this old wreck?' Piers grumbled.

'I chartered it, Piers, because it was extraordinarily cheap!' I informed him of the obvious reason. 'I'm ahead three hundred pounds per Member even before we get to St James,' I said as Piers noticed what Catchpole was doing.

'Don't you think you should tell him that isn't the toilet? Alan?' he asked me hysterically.

I paused before answering, 'I face a moral dilemma here, Piers. On the one hand I'd love to see Comrade Catchpole hurtling out of the plane, but on the other hand, I don't particularly wish to be sucked out after him.'

'Catchpole!' I raised my voice, reaching out my foot and prodded him with the toe of my shoe. 'I think there's someone in there,' I said as he turned and looked at me in confusion.

As Catchpole stumbled back to his seat, the Captain's voice

competed against the static on his intercom.

'Okaay, we're about to commence our descent to St James.' As we all clapped and cheered, he continued jovially, 'I hope you've all enjoyed this flight, because our motto is "service with a smile"; that's why so many famous people have flown Caribbean International: Buddy Holly, Otis Redding, Jim Reeves, Glenn Miller,' the pilot chortled. 'The old jokes are the best, folks.'

The planed suddenly hit some massive turbulence and began to buck and dip.

'Wheeyoo! Ride 'em Cowboy!' the arsehole exclaimed enthusiastically over the intercom as my drink spilled all over my lap.

I borrowed Piers's silk hankie from his breast pocket and mopped myself up, growling, 'God, I hate Americans! How can you have a nice day when there are Americans around?' I looked up and found the curvy and desirable Cyndy standing over me, a delicious pout of concern on her lips. 'Hello, you beautiful American,' I greeted her. 'I seem to have spilled my drink in my lap. Perhaps you'd like to . . . mop it up?'

'I'd really love to, but Captain Hirsch said, could you come into the cockpit right away,' she said.

I followed Cyndy to the flight deck, thinking, what is this? A sexual ploy? A special invitation to join the Mile High Club in the well-named cockpit?

Cyndy opened the cockpit door. Introducing me to Bobby and his co-pilot, Alex, she batted her eyelashes at the pilot and left the cramped flight deck.

'Hi, Al . . . Enjoying the flight?' The Captain grinned at me and waved a hand. At least, he waved an arm, but it ended in a hook.

'No.'

'Glad to hear it, Al,' Hirsch laughed. This confirmed my opinion that we were being piloted by a certified lunatic as did the bottle of brandy, complete with optic, at his left shoulder.

'Anything else?' I asked impatiently.

'Yup,' Hirsch nodded. 'Seems we got a little operational glitch relating to our ETA, Al,' he said incomprehensably.

'In English!' I demanded, tapping my foot.

'It's kinda hard to explain, Al . . .' the Captain said, removing his hand from the joystick and waving it vaguely in the air. The plane took a sudden nosedive.

'Well, break the habit of a lifetime and use your brain,' I said brusquely, replacing his hands on the controls.

'Alex, demonstrate. . . .' he ordered as Alex obediently clicked on the radio.

'This is Caribbean International Airways, Flight 001, requesting permission to land at St James International Airport,' Alex intoned into the mike.

A lackadaisical voice crackled back, 'This is St James Police Station. Is that you again, man? You just won't take no for an answer. We tell you, the airstrip closed till we harvest the sugar cane, everyone know that.'

I snatched the mike away from Alex and shouted into it, 'All right, listen to me. I am Alan B'Stard, Member of Parliament from England. My majority is four times the size of your entire population, and I'm visiting your island as the personal guest of President Okum-Martin, so stop playing silly buggers!'

A long cackle of laughter issued from the receiver. The voice went on, 'If President Lewis invited you, then Praise the Lord, it's a miracle. The poor old guy bin deaf, dumb and blind the last three years!'

'President Lewis!' I repeated into the mike. 'What are you talking about?'

'Lewis, that's the President's first name. We're all on first name terms here. This is a friendly island. Now push off, Honky!' the voice commanded.

'Listen, you stupid man. Your President's name is Lance. He's perfectly fit and healthy. I should know, I went to school with him,' I growled at the microphone.

Another roar of laughter resounded throughout the cockpit. 'Sounds like Lance has taken another Honky for a ride! Lance is the President's grandson. He's always pulling scams. Few years back, he nearly sold this entire island to the Disneyland people. That's what give the old man his stroke. Got out of bed one day, found Donald Duck in his swimming pool. Have a nice day!'

The radio went dead. I handed the mike back to Alex, tight-lipped and a touch panicked.

'There you go, Al. Looks like you been well and truly shafted,' Hirsch observed with glee.

'Thank you for your sympathy, Captain Hook. What a shame the Vietcong kept so little of you,' I shrieked as I pulled the hook from his arm and threw it on the floor.

'Then you've no right calling yourselves Caribbean International Airways,' I protested angrily.

I pushed my way out of the cockpit and returned to my seat.

I sat down next to Piers, muttering '. . . I'll really kill that double-dealing little con-merchant! He'll wish *he* was deaf, dumb and blind when I've finished with him.'

'Something the matter, Alan,' Piers piped up.

'Yes, the bank of St James has had an attack of premature liquidation . . . which means you're in a lot of trouble,' I said darkly, my mind working overtime.

'Me!!' Piers squealed.

'You've taken over a quarter of a million pounds in bankers' drafts from your colleagues under false pretences,' I accused him.

'But you've got the money,' he sputtered.

I agreed. 'I've got the money, but you're responsible for it, as Treasurer of The Friends of St James,' I explained.

'I'm the Secretary, not the Treasurer,' Piers contradicted.

'Don't you try those double-dealing, cheeseparing legalistic ploys with me!' I warned him, poking him in the ribs. 'When these good people sober up and find out how you've swindled them, they'll throw you off the plane . . . in mid-air!'

Piers hunched over and put his hands across his face, 'Oh my God, I'm going to die and I've never even been physically intimate with my fiancée.'

'Well, *I* have, and you aren't missing anything,' I snarled. 'Now, if you can get your mind off sex, I've just thought of a brilliant plan to save you! Give me your watch!' I demanded.

Piers opened his fingers and looked at me quizzically through them.

'Why?' he asked, clasping his left wrist protectively.

'Because I've always wanted a gold Rolex, that's why! Can you believe it? I'm about to save his miserable skin, and he's quibbling about a lousy watch! Keep it then, and time how long it takes you to hit the ground! I hope it's shock proof, that's all! ' I spat at him in disgust.

This had Piers really scared. He unlatched the Rolex from his wrist and handed it to me with, 'No, I want you to have it! '

'Thank you, Piers,' I put on the watch and admired it for a moment as I took a few deep breaths.

'Right. Follow me! ' I ordered him as I stood up.

Taking my flight bag from the overhead compartment I marched down the plane to the toilet at the back, passing row upon row of pickled parliamentarians. Piers obediently trotted along in my wake.

'We're going to pretend to hijack the plane,' I told Piers, who greeted my imaginative solution with petrified silence. I rummaged through the flight bag for suitable disguises, tossed Piers a tee-shirt and a pair of y-fronts, and told him to put them on. I put on another tee-shirt and stuffed my old shirt into the bag along with Piers's as he started to unzip his trousers, the silly-billy. Showing him what to do, I put the y-fronts over my head and arranged them so that I could see out of the fly. Piers followed suit as I wrenched the liquid soap dispenser from the lavatory wall. Flinging the flight bag over my shoulder, we burst through the door and back into the cabin.

Cyndy was canoodling with a couple of Members in the back row.

'. . . Yes, I took a Master's in political science at Cornell, but it doesn't do to come over too smart in this line of business. . .' She stopped short, startled, as I pulled her to her feet.

'Eek!' she squeaked, flailing about in my arms. Holding the soap dispenser aloft in one hand, I managed to press Cyndy's back against me. She whimpered as I shouted at the top of my voice in a Spanish accent, 'Hokay. This plane is bein hi-yacked by the People's Liberation Army of St Hames!'

Everyone started to turn around in their seats to stare at me. I brandished the soap dispenser at them threateningly, yelling, 'Hnobody turn around. We have grenades!'

'Do what he says!' Cyndy begged all the passengers. 'He's got a gun pressed into my back!'

That wasn't a gun. It was simply my way of saying hello, Dolly. I wiped the smile off my face. 'Everyone put their heads between their legs,' I commanded, and they all obeyed immediately. 'God, they did!' I whispered to Piers, impressed by the air of authority the soap dispenser had lent me. 'Hif hone of you Gringo pigs looks up, you're all Lassie Meaty Chunks, enriched with nourishing Member of Parliament!' I screamed.

'You can't kill me, I'm a Socialist. I'm on your side!' Catchpole got to his feet and turned to face me, a cowardly pleading look on his face.

'You're a Socialeest, I'm a Fasheest!' I proclaimed and pretended to start to hurl the 'grenade' at him.

Catchpole moaned, 'Oh, God!' and sank back down to his seat, replacing his head between his knees.

'Hokay. Hyou will all remove your wallets and pass them to

Comrade Juan,' I directed the passengers, whispering, 'That's you' to Piers.

Piers reluctantly started to make his way up the aisle. Every Member quickly passed his wallet over without looking up. He found a flight bag to carry the wallets in and I walked up the aisle alongside him, still clutching a struggling Cyndy.

'Quickly, you decadent pigs, if you hwish to see another dawn! ' I urged the Members, 'Hwe will avenge the Martyrs of the Battle of San. . . .' I paused to think, 'Ilav,' I concluded.

'Sanilav? ' Piers asked in a whisper out of the side of his mouth.

'My mind just went blank there for a second. Now I know how you feel all the time,' I whispered back.

We finally reached the front of the plane. I tossed the soap dispenser to Piers and grabbed the bag of wallets from him. I opened the door to the flight deck and pushed Cyndy through, shouting 'Long Live the glorious Octobre the Thirteenth Movement! ' as I entered the cockpit. After all, that was Mrs Thatcher's birthday.

Captain Hirsch and Alex looked at each other in fear as Cyndy and I burst in.

'It's the Sandinistas! ' Hirsch exclaimed, jumping up and getting a huge revolver out of his flight jacket.

I quickly ripped off my mask, proclaimimg 'It's okay, it's okay. It's me! ' I released Cyndy as a sign of goodwill.

'What in the name of Ollie H. North is going on, Al? ' Hirsch slumped back in his seat and rubbed his brow, putting his gun away with his other hand. Alex, fortunately, had put the plane on automatic pilot.

'It's far too complicated for an American to follow,' I assured the Captain. 'Look, I'll give you all the cash in this bag to forget this ever happened.'

Hirsch beamed and grabbed the bag from my hand, saying, 'You got it, Al.'

'And I'll just hang on to all these lovely bankers' drafts,' I added, patting my trouser pocket.

'Now, if you'll be so kind as to turn on the intercom,' I requested politely as Hirsch obeyed.

I put on my hijacker voice and shrieked into the mike, 'Fly this plane to Chile or I will blow the head off this English capitalist pig!'

I then said in my own voice, 'Don't listen to him, Captain Hirsch. He's bluffing. . .'

'Do as I say or we all die! This grenade is primed. I haaf only to remove my finger. . .' I continued my radio drama.

'This guy is good,' Hirsch whispered to Cyndy and Alex as he took over the mike, shouting, 'I'm changing course! Don't kill us!'

'I'll do anything, just don't remove your finger!' Cyndy entered into the spirit and yelled at the mike.

I took the mike from her and swung it round the flightdeck by its lead, grunting in my own voice, 'Uhh! Nnh! Quick, Captain, I've got the grenade. Grab them.' Then I swore in my Spanish accent, 'You will never take us halive! Come on, Juan, jump!'

'Oh God, no, the Emergency Exit!' My own voice gasped histrionically.

I turned on the hijack voice and screamed, 'For the glory of the counter-revolution! Aaaahhh!' I threw the microphone on the floor, shrieking.

'See that, Captain,' I observed in normal tones picking up the mike. 'The blighters have got a parachute!'

I opened the cockpit door and dragged Piers on to the flight deck with one arm. His hair was plastered down with liquid soap.

'Is the intercom off?' I whispered to Hirsch, who nodded.

'Quick, Piers. Get changed' I said urgently, ripping off the tee-shirt and putting my own shirt back on, I looked down at myself, considering my appearance, then ripped a couple of holes in the shirt with my teeth as Piers also donned his shirt.

'Now, hit me,' I commanded Piers.

'Why?' he asked, totally baffled.

'I need some signs of my heroic fight,' I explained, and Piers bashed me in the face rather harder than I had anticipated.

'I'll get you for this,' I promised him as blood began to gush from my nose. 'Okay, Bobby,' I prompted the Captain, who opened the door and walked inside the cabin.

'It's okay, folks,' he reassured the passengers in a soothing voice. 'It's all over, thanks to your Mr B'Stard. I knew some brave men in 'Nam, but this guy makes Rambo look like Sylvester Stallone!'

I entered the cabin humbly, with blood dripping on to my shirt. My fellow Friends all sat up in their seats and started to give me a swelling round of applause. Piers sneaked back into his seat without anyone noticing, and I held up my hands for silence.

'Thank you,' I acknowledged the Members' gratitude solemnly. 'It's all right, I only did my duty. After all, I brought you out here,' I put on an air of false regret and sighed, 'I'm just sorry things went so drastically wrong: obviously St James is not a safe investment prospect.'

I frowned and shook my head at the ensuing cries of 'Not your fault!' and 'Well done, B'Stard!' from the other passengers and again raised my hands for silence.

'But I'm afraid that when the hijackers parachuted out of the plane, they took all our wallets with them. So all the bankers' drafts we brought to deposit in St James are now in the hands of desperate terrorists,' I confessed.

'To hell with the money. You're a hero, B'Stard!' Catchpole stood up and declared warmly.

All the other Members concurred: 'That's right, you saved our lives!' 'The money doesn't matter!' 'Thank God we're safe! ' It was a really gratifying moment.

Piers, who had been primed by me in the cockpit, stood up and declared, 'Anyway, we're all insured, aren't we? ' Those who weren't groaned, those who were looked vastly relieved.

'I didn't take out any insurance. I was so confident,' I admitted ruefully, then shrugged, 'Well, that's a hundred thousand down the drain. . ..'

'We can't let Alan lose all that, can we? ' Piers asked The Friends of St James. 'I propose we have a collection for him when we get back. All in favour? '

Eventually everyone's hand went up, though some with more reluctance than others. I quickly noted their owners for future reference.

'Thank you, I'm very touched,' I said in a trembling voice. Wiping the tears from my eyes, I sat down beside Piers and promised, 'If that collection tops ten grand, you can have your watch back. . . .'

CHAPTER SIX

THREE LINE WHIPPING

We Members of Parliament lead extrememly stressful lives, and as medical opinion is unanimous that too much work and too little exercise is the surest way to guarantee a premature death, I decided to take some time off and put myself in the hands of a specialist before it was too late.

I took a taxi to Islington on a spanking fine summer evening and arrived at Mrs Selway's beautiful Georgian house just in time for my appointment. Mrs Selway is a charming professional lady who always manages to come up with just the right tonic to recharge my batteries and I was greatly looking forward to our consultation.

'My dear, how delightful. I'm so pleased you could find the time,' she greeted me with her usual hospitality as she opened the door.

I kissed her on both cheeks, saying warmly, 'My pleasure absolutely, Mrs Selway.'

'And how is your lovely wife? ' she inquired politely as she led me through her tastefully decorated corridor.

'No idea, haven't seen her for days,' I replied.

'It's not easy to make a marriage work these days, but I can see you have the secret,' Mrs Selway said, patting my hand. 'I've put you in the pink room,' she smiled.

'My favourite,' I approved, as I went up the stairs.

On the bed in the pink room was just what the doctor ordered. She looked up from the television and smiled sweetly at me as I entered the room.

'Hello,' I greeted her, very much taken by her appearance, especially the teacher's gown and the mortar board which was perched pertly on her head.

'Bonjour, my name is Chantelle, I'm your new French mistress,' she introduced herself, switching off the television. 'You must be Mr B.?'

'Yes,' I acknowledged feeling her thighs and breasts for muscle tone, 'but please call me Piers. . .'

She smiled at me and commented, 'That's a nice name.'

'Yes. It isn't mine, of course. . .'

'Me neither,' she confessed as I removed my jacket and began to unbutton my shirt. She giggled. 'Mrs Selway told me what you like. . . you naughty boy!' She shook her finger at me and pursed her sexy lips in mock disapproval.

'I find it helps me to unwind after a long sitting,' I explained with a little shrug. I went to examine the rack of whips and canes next to the bed and took my pick.

'Mmm, this is a nice whippy one,' I said, testing a cane in the air. I put it on the bed, and got out of my trousers and shoes.

'I told you what would happen if you failed your French oral again,' Chantelle said as I bent over to remove my socks.

'What? ' Jesus!! Ouch!' I exclaimed as she swiped me really hard on the bum with the cane. The pain was excrutiating. I beat a retreat to the other side of the bed, but Chantelle continued to lash at me with the cane. 'That hurts! Stop it!' I ordered.

'It's meant to hurt, you silly boy!' She smiled and flailed the thing at me again.

'You stupid trollop!' I grabbed her arm and took the cane away from her. 'I'm not a masochist. I'm a sadist! I pay to beat you!'

'I'm sorry,' The silly bitch began to cry. 'I'm new here.'

I took Chantelle in my arms to soothe away her tears. I tickled her gently to make her laugh, and when she was her cheerful self again, I gave her a good thrashing.

I eventually fell asleep on my stomach on top of the bedclothes. It was the only comfortable position for my still-smarting bum.

A uniformed policeman bursting through the door at some ungodly hour wakened me with a jolt.

'Here, there's one in here's got more stripes than you, Sarge!' he shouted and yelled at me, 'All right, you pevert! Downstairs. Now!'

Oh God. Just what I needed to make my life complete. A bust. I considered a quick escape through the window, but the policeman was still glaring at me from the doorway, anticipating my desire for a hasty departure.

Groaning, I wrapped the sheet round myself and reluctantly allowed the policeman to usher me down the stairs to join Mrs Selway's other guests and a handful of policemen who were guarding them in the hallway.

I announced to no one in particular, 'I shouldn't be here at all. I'm from the Good Food Guide. Terrible mix-up at the office. . . .'

Very oddly, none of the other clients seemed particularly nervous or frightened. They looked more annoyed than anything else.

One man old enough to be Sir Stephen's father addressed me, 'What a damn bore these interruptions are. . . takes me long enough to get my engine running as it is. . . .'

'Yes, it must be pretty clapped out, if the bodywork's anything to go by,' I couldn't help quipping.

Another portly client, dressed only in boxer shorts, peered at the old gent closely and said, 'Cyril, I didn't know you were a member here, old boy!'

Cyril raised his eyebrows and nodded, 'Yes, I've been coming here for years. . . .'

'So to speak!' They both laughed. 'Congrats on your elevation to the Court of Appeal, by the way,' the boxer-shorted individual said and then he looked at me. 'I say, it's B'Stard, isn't it? ' he declared.

'Not necessarily. . . .' I said cautiously, backing away.

'Yes, of course it is! You did very well with your Private Member's Bill arming the police,' the portly man congratulated me as a very agitated Mrs Selway appeared from the lounge accompanied by an angry-looking Inspector.

'I'm most terribly sorry, gentlemen,' she said sadly to her clients. 'Inspector Radford here is new, and apparently no one has explained our special relationship with the local force. . . .'

'If you're implying, Madam, that some nod and wink deal has been in operation between my nick and your bawdy house! ' Inspector Radford rocked back on his heels and looked down his nose at Mrs Selway.

'Of course it has! ' It's been that way for years,' she insisted in a sexy voice.

'You realise I could do you for that! ' Radford threatened, waggling his finger at her.

'And I expect she'd give you a discount,' I joked, beginning to enjoy myself.

Radford scowled at me and then scowled at all of us in general as he got out his notebook. 'All right, sleazebags, names and addresses. . . .'

Cyril introduced himself: 'Right Honourable Sir Cyril Haversham-Armstrong, Court of Appeal, and this is Major General Ralph Murdo McDonald, KCMG, KCVO, DSO, Ministry of Defence.' He indicated a very embarrassed-looking man on his left.

'If you think I'm going to waste ink writing down this crap! ' Radford stopped writing. 'Now, let's have your real name,' he said to me.

'Piers Fletcher-Dervish, MP, House of Commons,' I replied promptly.

'I told you! ' Radford warned loudly.

'Before you go on, Inspector. Let me show you this,' the portly man said. He reached into the waistband of his boxer shorts and withdrew a piece of plastic. 'My warrant card,' he said, offering it to the Inspector.

' "Commander Stapleton, Vice Squad" ! ' Radford read aloud. 'That'll do nicely, Sir,' he said limply, handing the card back to the Commander.

Radford shooed his confused force out of the front door, announcing heartily, 'All right, lads, there seems to have been an administrative cock-up here. . . .'

'What a facility you have for the telling phrase, Inspector,' I said to his departing back.

'What a cock-up, indeed,' I repeated to myself as I wearily went back upstairs to the pink room for a little rest. I turned on the television as I climbed gingerly back into bed. 'Good Morning Britain' was just starting on TV A.M. and Jane Irving was previewing the morning's show.

'. . .And in a few minutes time, we'll have Bob Crippen MP and Alan B'Stard MP in the studio to discuss the implications of last night's crucial by-election. But first, Popeye. . . .'

'Oh, shit! ' I said as her words sank in, I was so whacked that the interview had completely slipped my mind. I jumped out of bed and raced to get my clothes out of the wardrobe.

Chantelle, gagged and bound, was in there, too, of course.

'Hmmpphhh, hmmpphhh! ' she exclaimed through her gag, glaring at me. 'That'll teach you to beat up your clients! ' I said to her as I shut the wardrobe door.

Fortunately, Islington is only a couple of miles from TV A.M.'s studios, and I could just make the interview in time if I found a taxi right away.

I was lucky.

'TV A.M. double double quick! ' I urged the driver as I clambered into the back of his cab.

'I hope you're not asking me to exceed the speed limit?' the cabby asked jocosely as he put the meter on.

'Just bloody well drive!' I snarled as the cab moved off sedately.

I had to perch uncomfortably on the edge of the seat because of my throbbing bottom. I couldn't help wincing every time we turned a corner sharply.

'Sit well back in your seat if you wouldn't mind, chief, in case I have to make an emergency stop,' the driver said to me over his shoulder.

'I'll sit as I choose! Just mind your own business and put your horrible common foot down!' I said, I had only five minutes left.

The taxi made an emergency stop. I fell on the floor.

'The Metropolitan Hackney Carriage office would have my badge if I didn't attend to passengers' safety at all times,' the driver said, crossing his arms.

'All right,' I said, and sat well back into the seat just to get the officious little sod driving again. 'I'm sitting comfortably. Now, will you begin, you irritating little virus!'

The cab drove off slowly. A second later the driver leaned through the partition and said gleefully, 'I know why you were perching on the edge of your seat! You've been for a bit of hanky spanky at Mrs Selway's famous knocking emporium!' I slammed the partition shut, but the cabby reopened it, saying, 'Nothing to be ashamed of, Mrs Selway's is a landmark of old London. It's even one of the runs on the Knowledge now: how do you get from Mrs Selway's to the Middlesex Hospital Clap Clinic?'

We finally arrived at the studio forecourt, with no time at all to spare. I wouldn't even be able to have a much-needed shave and wash.

Feeling really rumpled and depressed, I rushed out of the taxi.

'Oy! ' I heard the cabby call after me as I entered the building, 'I didn't expect a tip, but. . . ! '

I didn't turn back since I didn't have the time to pay him anyway.

I quicky found the right studio and a floor assistant brought me straight on to the set. Jane Irving was sitting on her sofa, dressed entirely in blinding pink and watching an advert on the monitor.

'You're cutting it fine, B'Stard. . . whose bed did you oversleep in, then? ' asked Crippen cutely as he crept up next to me and stubbed his fag out on the floor.

'You're on right after the break,' the floor manager said. 'Is there anything you need? '

'More cushions,' I demand, sitting on the chair he led me to.

The floor manager sent his assistant for another cushion and a make-up girl applied powder to my face and combed my hair, tuttutting all the while. The floor assistant returned with a cushion, which I slid under my sore botty as the floor manager gave the five second countdown with his fingers.

In a sudden panic, I grabbed some menial's arm as he passed and asked, 'Who won the by-election? '

'What by-election? ' he asked, shrugging me off.

We were on air.

'Yesterday's by-election posed an important challenge to all political parties. In the studio this morning we have Alan B'Stard, Conservative MP for Haltemprice and Bob Crippen, Labour Member for Brammall,' Jane Irving turned her face to me and smacked her lips, 'Well, Alan, all the pundits said that this by-election, the first in a Tory marginal since a controversial Budget, would be an important hurdle for the Government.' I nodded sagely as she continued, 'Were you surprised by the result? '

I decided Jane's question could only mean that the Tories had lost the seat. I hedged confidently, 'Not really. . . were you, Bob? '

'Surprised? ' Crippen raised his eyebrows at the camera, 'I was completely gobstruck. It was a bolt from the blue! '

'Of course it was,' I agreed with urbanity. 'But it was a predictable one, so I wasn't really surprised.'

'But to get down to the specifics. . .' Jane persisted, boringly.

'Look, Jane, I think people have had enough of politics this year,' I patted Jane on the knee in an avuncular fashion. Her complexion grew even more healthy-looking as she removed my hand. I continued, 'Let us talk about what really matters: how is Anne Diamond's lovely little baby doing? '

'We're here to talk about the by-election result, not some media brat,' Crippen had the gall to interrupt me. He leaned forward and asked, 'Unless you don't know the result, B'Stard.'

'I not know the result! That's outrageous! I charged.

'What was it then? ' The bastard had the nerve to ask.

'I'm not going to be browbeaten by some bald-headed crypto-Stalinist! ' I was so affronted I could scarcely speak.

'All right, you ask him, Jane,' Crippen said, pointing at her. Jane giggled, embarrassed.

'I'm sure you must know the result Alan? ' she pestered.

'Yes, of course, I nodded. 'Labour. . . came second,' I changed course as the other two laughed. 'And we held the seat, of course. It was a foregone conclusion. . . .'

'Actually, it was a surprise victory for the S.D.P.' Jane said, taking visible pleasure in correcting me.

I flipped. 'That's it. Get me up early and ask trick questions. Now I know how Denis Healy felt! ' I stood up and shouted as I unclipped the microphone and threw it on the floor.

'Don't Mrs Selway have a newspaper delivered? ' Crippen laughed after me as I stormed off the set.

I left the studio in a foul mood and made for the toilet to

compose myself. Unfortunately for me, the floor manager was just rezipping himself as I entered. He looked at me and was unable to restrain his stupid laughter. I looked at myself gloomily in the mirror and was retying my tie as someone else came in.

'Oy, oy! Now I know what MP stands for. . . "Monumental Prat" ! ' this someone said.

I turned round angrily to confront whoever it was. It was the taxi driver, who was a stunted little oik of about four feet tall.

'How dare you, you little. . .'

'Heightist' the mini-cabby accused as he aimed a short stream of pee into the urinal. 'I had to hang about. You didn't pay my fare, so I came in and watched you on the set in Reception. It was worth £3.50 of anybody's money, so the ride's on me.' He zipped up his fly, continuing to abuse me. 'Blimey, I feel almost sorry for you, when Maggie finds out about this morning, I shouldn't be surprised if there's another by-election called in your constituency! '

'Shut up! '

'Fancy not even knowing the result! ' he laughed at me. 'I would have told you if you'd asked me nicely. But you didn't want to hear my vulgar northern accent. . .' the midget continued as he washed his hands.

'Shut up, or I'll hit you! ' I promised him.

'Oh, yeah, very brave, hit a man of diminished stature, with a dicky heart to boot. Just goes to show, any old tosspot can become a Tory MP if he knows what palms to grease! ' he taunted me beyond my point of endurance.

Quivering with rage, I threatened, 'I'm warning you! '

But the little bastard replied, 'I've always wanted to meet a surviving brain transplant donor. . .'

'That does it! ' I announced. I picked him up by his lapels to give him a really good shake, accidentally banging his head on the towel dispenser.

The fellow immediately went unconscious on me. Shocked, I

let him slip down the wall to the floor. He left a bright trail of blood on the white tiles.

'Come on, get up, you Pinko runt!' I said, kicking him gently to rouse him. But he didn't stir. 'Come on. Get up! Please!'

Worried now, I crouched down and put my ear to the cabby's chest. Nada. 'Oh Christ, I said out loud. 'That's all I need first thing on a Friday morning. A dead dwarf!'

Some days it just doesn't pay to get out of bed, I reflected as I heaved the body out of the loo window and climbed out the small aperture myself.

I dragged the corpse to the taxi and stuffed it into the boot, thinking that things could be worse. I might have accidentally topped a sumo wrestler. Then I'd really be hard pressed to dispose of the body. This one was a piece of cake in comparison. It didn't weigh more than a couple of sacks of potatoes and fitted so neatly into the boot space with room to spare. I removed the car keys from the defunct driver's pocket and, shutting the boot and locking it, I let myself into the cab and started it up.

I couldn't figure out, though, how to turn the blasted 'For Hire' sign off, so my progress was impeded by various prospective passengers attempting to hail me and generally getting in my way. Nearing Westminster, I was forced to stop at a red light. Some fool attempted to open the passenger door, saying 'Albert Hall'.

'Fred Housego, pleased to meet you,' I said pleasantly as the lights turned green and I sped off, probably wrenching off his arm in the process.

I decided to go the House, to create an alibi in case my as yet unthought-out plans went awry. I parked on a nearby meter and proceeded to my office.

Piers and Sir Stephen were already there, looking as bleary-eyed and dishevelled as I felt.

'Oh, do I know you? Yes, it's Alan thingy, isn't it? ' Piers said sarcastically.

'Spare me your pathetic attempts at humour, Piers,' I said, sitting down heavily in my chair.

'And where were you last night when we were voting on the Bill to recriminalise prostitution? ' Sir Stephen asked in a portentous manner. What a bore he is for attention to detail.

'I was paired. . . .' I excused myself.

'Yes, with one of Mrs Selway's girls, no doubt! ' Sir Stephen snorted. 'Hypocrite! '

'*Au contraire*, I'd only be a hypocrite if I had voted last night. I like brothels; you don't have to pretend to respect women,' I replied in all honesty.

'The Chief Whip's out for your blood, you know,' Piers cautioned me in a gleeful tone.

'And everyone's talking about what an arse you made of yourself on television this morning. You've let us all down, B'Stard. I'm disappointed in you.' He levelled a sad gaze at me, looking just like a dying bloodhound.

'Do you think I give an orang-utang's for the opinion of a man with a plastic drainpipe where his colon should be? ' I asked him, deliberately aiming below the belt.

'You'll be old one day, B'Stard,' Sir Stephen commented in a hurt voice.

'But I shan't be bionic! ' I vowed as he stood up and shuffled to the door with the remains of his dignity.

'Off to his Harley Street Plumber, no doubt,' I said as the door closed behind him.

I turned to Piers and wheedled, 'Piers, will you do me a small favour? '

'That depends. . . .' Piers replied, cagily.

'I've got a taxi waiting downstairs. . . .'

'And you want me to go pay the driver as usual,' he sighed as he searched his pockets for change.

'Don't try to anticipate me, you don't have the wit,' I informed him, adding, 'I want you to drive the taxi out into the country, somewhere secluded, and set fire to it.'

'Why?' Piers asked in amazement.

'Because it's a very old taxi and I don't need it anymore,' I offered him an explanation he'd fall for. 'Here are the keys,' I said, dangling them in front of his nose.

'I don't want to,' he whined and backed away from me.

'What? Why not? Give me a good reason.' I tried my usual intimidation tactics, but to no avail.

'Taxis aren't biodegradable. It would upset the wildlife,' Piers excused himself lamely.

'Poor little bunnies,' I snarled, and looked at him through hooded eyes which is something I do rather well. 'Well, if you won't do a simple favour for your best friend. . . .' I let the thought dangle.

'I wouldn't call setting fire to a taxi exactly a simple favour,' he complained in his usual niggling fashion.

'Of course it's simple. It's as simple as you! All you need is a can of petrol and a box of matches!' He scowled at me, shaking his head. 'Never mind, I'll do it myself! Give me your wallet!' I demanded, snapping my fingers at him.

'Why?' Piers said, his hand covering his jacket pocket protectively.

'You don't expect me to pay my own fare back from the middle of nowhere after I've disposed of the taxi for you?' I exclaimed indignantly.

'Oh sorry, Alan,' Piers apologised, handing me his wallet.

'That's better,' I cooed at him. I went to the coatstand and picked up a new-looking barbour jacket from it, 'Is this yours, Piers?'

'Yes,' he exclaimed proudly. 'It's new. Do you want to borrow it?'

'Waterproof, is it?' I asked as I pretended to examine the naff thing.

'Yes, it's impregnated with wax. . . .'

'Let's see how it copes with old Father Thames,' I said as I opened the window and threw the jacket out, just to teach him a little lesson.

The garage attendant charged me five pounds for an empty tin, the shyster. I filled it with five litres of two-star and bought two boxes of Swan Vestas and ten Woodbines to throw him off the track.

Then I raced back to the taxi, threw the packet of fags away and put the petrol on the floor of the driver's compartment, covering it with a mangy old scarf I found on the seat.

I crossed Westminster Bridge on my way out of London to find a secluded enough spot to set fire to the taxi without fear of detection. The 'For Hire' sign on the top of the cab was still alight. At least ten people tried to flag me down, but I ignored them. What's the matter with people these days, anyway? Don't they know what feet were invented for?

Half-way down Denmark Hill a stupid policeman blocked my path by standing in the middle of the road. He motioned me to stop and I really thought my goose was cooked.

'Yes, Officer?' I asked meekly.

The Police Officer pointed to the side of the road. A black Jag had been in a collision with a purple Datsun. Its chauffeur and the Datsun's petrified driver were exchanging insurance details on the pavement. The Jag's three uninjured passengers were collecting their briefcases and things from the boot. One was a burly-looking man with a vigilant air, the other two were all too familiar; the Prime Minister and the Chief Whip.

'Dulwich,' the policeman said.

I quickly considered my options. I could drop dead. Or I

could ignore the policeman and carry on, in which case he'd give chase and find the dead dwarf in the boot. Or I could bluff it out.

I grabbed the scarf and swiftly tied it around as much of my face as I could so they wouldn't recognise me and pushed the glass partition shut.

My three passengers got in, and off we went. Everything went smoothly until the man who must be Maggie's minder opened the partition to give me directions.

'. . .and how does Dennis react to the idea of your running for a fourth term? ' The Chief Whip was asking.

'He's less then completely enamoured. Threatening to vote Monster Raving Loony. . . .' Maggie barked a short laugh.

'Mind you, many more Tory performances like B'Stard's this morning and there might not be a fourth,' the Chief Whip commented and I could feel my face turning bright red.

'Yes, what are we going to do about him, Chief Whip? ' Maggie asked him in a concerned fashion. 'It was quite the worst television appearance since Michael Foot hung up his welding spectacles,' she said unfairly.

'And he failed to respond to a three-line whip last night! He seems to think that just because he's got the largest majority in the House he's immune to discipline! ' the Chief Whip said, his voice shaking with rage. 'Well, tomorrow I intend to haul him over the coals. . . .'

I went for broke and adopted a broad Northern accent. 'Pardon the intrusion,' I said, 'but I saw him on telly this morning, and I think he did champion! ' I said enthusiastically.

'Do you mind!! I don't believe the Prime Minister intended to include you in her conversation,' the Chief Whip told me rudely, and Maggie's minder started to close the partition.

'No,' Maggie said restraining him, 'I'm interested in hearing what the man in the street has to say.'

'And you're in the right place, ma'am,' I assured her. ' 'Cos the man in the street frequently becomes the man in my cab. In fact, you're being driven by a one-man opinion poll! And seventy-two per cent of my passengers say that Alan B'Stard's all right! He speaks his mind, says what us decent working chaps. . . er, folk. . . want to hear. I mean, didn't he get that law through what give the police their guns? Right! Granted he seemed a bit nervy on the telly this morning, but I reckon he was just trying to wind that Commie Crippen up! ' I defended myself brilliantly.

'Thank you for sharing your political insights with us,' the Chief Whip said in a patronising manner and shut the divider. 'Now, about the committee arrangements. . .' I overheard him continue.

I reopened the divider and observed, 'I've always been Labour in the past, never cared for them old-fashioned toffee-nosed Tories like Sir Stephen Baxter. But with ordinary lads like B'Stard coming through, you'll get my vote, and hundreds of other ignorant, working-class cabbies feel the same way! ' I assured them with relish.

'We'd have got more work done if we'd taken a bus,' the Chief Whip complained.

A few minutes later we arrived at Maggie's new house and I drew up behind Dennis's Roller. The PM and the Chief Whip walked up the driveway to the house as the minder got out his wallet.

'Oy, mouthie,' the detective said, noting the 'For Hire' sign on, 'You know it's illegal to pick up fares without turning your meter on? '

Fares? ' I retorted. 'I wouldn't charge that wonderful woman a brass farthing, even if my family was starving. Which, of course it isn't, because us small business folk are flourishing under her wise government.'

'Crawler,' the minder said, putting his wallet away.

I shouted at him as I drove off, 'That don't mean I weren't

expecting a decent tip! ' I think that's thrown her off the scent, I said to myself.

I made my way out into the sticks of Kent without further ado, I had to choose a place that wasn't too far to walk to a railway station, so, as I passed a sign indicating 'Pratts Bottom Railway Station, I began to look seriously for a little-used country lane or unbeaten track. It wasn't too difficult to find a suitable spot.

I stopped the cab, got out my petrol tin and poured its contents all over the car. Suddenly I heard a sound. I turned around. A man on horseback was spying on me.

'Can't bear to have a dirty bonnet,' I said gaily, getting out my handkerchief and polishing the taxi with it as though what I'd poured on it had been Turtle Wax.

About three miles further down the main road I spied a track leading to what looked like a large body of water. As I'd used up all the petrol, I had to dispose of the damned taxi another way. A sign warned, 'Deep Water. No lifeguard on duty'. Just the ticket.

I got out of the taxi, leaving the handbrake off, and began to push the wretched thing to the water's edge. Just as I'd got about a yard from the water, a frogman popped up not ten feet away from me.

Thinking quickly, I opened the bonnet of the cab. 'Overheating, I announced to the frogman. 'Got to wait for it to cool down before I can top up the radiator.'

The frogman waved at me and disappeared below the surface of the water again, Damn.

I drove the taxi another few miles down quite a number of seemingly deserted lanes, but to no avail. I was feeling very cross and absolutely exhausted. 'Stupid over-populated county,' I snarled to myself. 'In Yorkshire it'd be a piece of pudding,' I said, looking at my watch. A huge yawn overtook me and I completely lost control of the taxi.

I careered straight into a shed, the cab was a write-off, but my seatbelt had protected me from harm, except I'd bumped my head and blood was trickling down my face. I couldn't have been more pleased.

I got out of the driver's seat and, checking that no more nosy parkers were lurking around this time, I opened the boot and pulled the corpse out.

I dragged the body round to the front of the taxi and propped it up behind the steering wheel. I then got into the back of the cab and arranged myself in an unconscious position and waited to be discovered.

I must have fallen asleep. It was already dark when I heard noises. I sneaked a look out of the window. There was a patrol car containing two policemen, 'About time,' I whispered to myself and resumed my unconscious pose.

One of the patrolmen opened the passenger door. 'Are you all right, sir?' he asked me solicitously.

'Nnnnhh. . . ' I moaned softly.

The policeman waved smelling salts under my nose. 'Mnn, no more gorgonzola for me, I'm stuffed,' I said, feigning delirium.

'This one's coming round,' the policeman shouted to his mate. I allowed him to help me to a sitting position, groaning in my pain.

An ambulance soon arrived. I began to give my statement to the policeman as one of the ambulance attendants attempted to revive the corpse.

'I was at TV A.M. . . .' I started.

'I thought it was you,' the silly bugger sniggered.

I glared at him and continued with dignity, 'I finished my interview, and asked him to take me back to my Chelsea *pied à terre*. Suddenly he went mad, started driving through red lights, shouting and cursing me and the Conservative Party! I tried to throw myself out, but there are childproof locks on the door! He

141

was obviously insane. . . and now he's dead. Better dead I suppose than life in a lunatic asylum. . . .'

As if on cue, the cabby came round at this point, and leaped at me, his hands encircling my throat, but the patrolman easily restrained the little sod.

'Now, take it easy, shorty. You're still concussed,' an ambulance attendant said to him.

'And look at the state of my cab!' the dwarf ranted on.

'All right, all right,' a policeman said, patting the cabby on the top of his ugly head. 'Come on, let's all go back to the nick and sort it out there.'

'There's nothing to sort out, officer. You have my statement, who are you going to believe? The Conservative member of Parliament with the largest majority in the House of Commons, or this foul-mouthed ignorant stunted little taxi driver? ' I asked them reasonably. 'If I were you, I would take this homunculus back to the police station and have him tested for drugs,' I suggested.

The two policemen looked at each other, then they looked at me and the cabby. Reaching a wordless agreement, they picked the midget up by the armpits and marched him to the patrol car, his legs thrashing the air as they went.

'What do you think you're doing to me? You can't believe all that old toot! ' the cabby shouted indignantly as the policemen forced him into the car. As they drove away I could still see his little mouth opening and shutting, still carrying on his pointless tirade.

'If you'd like to come with us, sir, we'll take you to Basildon General to get that wound dressed,' one of the ambulance men offered, taking my arm.

I shrugged him off. 'You don't think I'd set foot inside a National Health Service Hospital after ten years of Government cut-backs? Take me to Harley Street,' I ordered as I entered the rear door of the ambulance.

I slept like a log that night after my ordeal and arrived at my office earlier than usual the next morning, refreshed and ready for action.

Sir Stephen glared at me as I entered the office, 'Ah, B'Stard! Come to clear your desk out, have you? ' he asked in a superior voice.

'What? ' I asked distractedly and sat down at my desk to read the newspaper.

'The Chief Whip was in here earlier, looking for you. . . but you weren't here,' Sir Stephen clucked at me like a hen and continued, 'That's three times you've let me down in two days. He left muttering about breaches of discipline. If I were you I'd try to land a few directorships while you still have MP after your name,' he admonished me, feebly slapping his desk.

'But I've got the biggest majority in the House. What can he do to me? ' I yawned and examined my fingernails.

'He can have you thrown out of the Party; he can promote you and send you to Ulster. He can. . . .' He spluttered as the Chief Whip entered the room.

'Ah, Chief Whip, just the man,' I said chirpily. 'Perhaps you can give me some advice? I've just been left twenty thousand pounds by a distant aunt, and fortunately, as I'm extremly wealthy and don't need the money, I've decided to donate it to your favourite charity. And, being an anti-bureaucratic sort of chap, I thought "cut out the red tape, give it to the good old Chief Whip in his hand and let him get on with it." ' I smiled and reached into my breast pocket for my chequebook.

'Cut the crap, B'Stard,' the Chief Whip shouted, unimpressed. 'I don't like you, I've never liked you, and I don't wish to spend any more time in your company than is absolutely necessary. I think your behaviour over the last days has been execrable, and if it were up to me, you'd become an unfortunate hiccough in the otherwise downward trend of unemployment statistics,' he raged. 'The Prime Minister, however, seems to rather like you. I suppose even the greatest post-war leader this country has had is entitled to one lapse of judgement,' he concluded sadly.

Sir Stephen gasped in astonishment. 'Margaret likes him!'

I put on my northern cabby voice and said, 'I don't know, happen it's good for her to keep in touch with the man in the street, eh, Chief Whip?'

The sound of the Chief Whip's jaw hitting the tiles echoed around the Palace of Westminster. I shall cherish the memory.

CHAPTER SEVEN

BAA BAA BLACKSHEEP

I was beginning to think Beatrice was a two-faced bitch. Ever since Sarah and I had got back together again, Beatrice had been out to bring me to heel. Carp, carp, carp, every step of the way. Although I do like masterful women, Ms Bossy Boots's tactics were really below the belt. Although I hadn't had much spare time to court her lately, I felt this was unfair treatment. If she wanted to get to grips with me, then she knew how to reach me for a hands-on experience that neither of us would be likely to forget. Instead, she had sicked that rabid bull terrier, my father-in-law on to me yet again, and there I was, one lovely Saturday morning, just before my first anniversary as Member of Parliament, imprisoned in my own sitting room by that deadly bore who said he was speaking on behalf of both of them. He was giving me a bollocking *sauvage* and I was defending myself as persuasively as I could, while watching him freeload my best brandy.

'You can't drop me as your Member of Parliament just because I missed a meeting of the local party,' I asserted myself, narrowing my eyes at him over my snifter.

'Since you were elected, you've missed every meeting of the local party! In fact, we're running a "Spot the MP" competition in the constituency newsletter. Anyone who sees you in Haltemprice wins a fiver,' Roland exaggerated wildly. He knew full well that his dear daughter had made it part of our resealed marriage pact that I stay in London as much as possible, and I was keeping my side of the deal to the best of my ability.

'But there are more important things for an MP to do than swan around the constituency pressing the flesh.' I reminded him of my onerous responsibilities at Westminster.

'Agreed,' Roland nodded, 'and you don't do any of those things either. You never hold surgeries; you never ask questions in the House unless in the furtherance of your own profit; you throw away constituents' letters, and use your secretarial allowance to run your Bentley. You refuse to meet deputations; you fail to support local events; you take absolutely no interest in local industry. . . .' That tattletale Beatrice had really put the wind up the old fart's sails.

'All right, I admit it. I'm not perfect,' I said simply and walked over to the sideboard to take a Havana cigar from my humidor.

'I blame myself,' Roland said, shaking his head sadly. 'Years ago, we were offered Leon Brittan as our MP, and I rejected him because he was Jewish. But after you, I won't even demur if Central Office foist a darkie on us!'

'Look, Roland,' I sighed. This was really becoming an uphill struggle. 'Have a cigar. In fact, have two.' I offered him the humidor. Roland took two cigars, a giant Churchill to smoke now and a Lew Grade, which he slipped into his sock for later. 'I know we haven't always seen eye to eye. . . well, never,' I attempted to placate the bastard. 'But your personal antipathy towards me. . . .'

'Hatred,' he interrupted.

'. . . shouldn't be allowed wholly to cloud the issue,' I stated as I lit my cigar. 'How do the other members of the executive feel about me?'

'Who knows? Who cares?' Roland shrugged. 'I run Haltemprice Conservative Association. My executive council thinks what I tell them to think!' He tapped his chest with pride, continuing, 'In that respect it's a perfect miniature of Mrs Thatcher's cabinet.'

Sarah came in with a clutch of overstuffed carrier bags from a morning's looting of York's best designer shops. I was grateful for the interruption to this tedious coversation.

'Oh, hello, Daddy,' She kissed her father on the cheek. 'Will you stay for something to eat?'

I groaned, but he shook his head, declaring, 'Not hungry. Just chewed up and spat out your husband.' He barked a short laugh and announced ominously, 'I'm leaving, but it's him that's on his way out.'

Roland's threat had clouded my day. I went to the bedroom to have a lie down and a quiet think, but Sarah followed me upstairs with her purchases.

'Do you think he's serious about sacking me?' I asked as she slipped her dress over her head and tried on a new tee-shirt.

'Daddy's always serious. Compared to him P.W. Botha's an old softy,' Sarah said distractedly, smoothing down her hair and examining herself in the full length mirror in the dressing room. 'Will you try to find another constituency, or will you give up politics and concentrate on being a full-time spiv?' she asked, her eyes locking with mine in the mirror.

'Neither!' I assured her with a glare. 'I'll be MP for Haltemprice well into the next century! I intend to go on and on!'

'I bet you say that to all the girls. . . .' she tittered, trying on a new bikini top.

'There's a month before the next executive council meeting, that's time enough to enhance my reputation. . . .' I thought aloud.

'Can one enhance what doesn't exist?' She asked archly, admiring her boobs.

'Of course, this is real politics, not real life,' I instructed her as I also admired her boobs. 'A few large donations to popular charities, some well-publicised appearances at local events, and I'll soon be everyone's blue-eyed boy again,' I stated casually.

'Not Daddy's,' she contradicted as she struggled into the bikini bottoms.

'He has only one vote,' I shrugged, 'I'll need your help, though. A politician isn't dressed without a loving wife on his arm. We'll have to be seen at charity functions, county shows, we'll have to visit geriatric wards, kiss babies. It's a nauseating prospect, but it goes down well with the plebs,' I informed her.

'Who goes down well?' Sarah was paying more attention to the shape of her profile than the needs of her husband.

Actually, the shape of her profile was looking pretty good to me too at the moment. 'Sarah, all this dressing and undressing is very distracting. . . .' I implied in a seductive tone.

'Oh, am I turning you on?' she asked breezily.

'Well, as Kipling probably said, "Down in the jungle, something stirred",' I replied, making a grab for her.

She batted me away, saying, 'I'm sorry if I've given you a Rudyard-on, Alan, but don't let's spoil a perfectly stable marriage by trying to reintroduce sex into it.'

Stung, I countered, 'I'm not the one giving the impromptu strip show!'

'I'm simply trying on all the beachwear you've just paid for,' the bitch said as she wrapped a new sarong around her shapely body. 'I don't want to arrive in Greece to find my bikinis are too loose.'

'Greece!' I repeated. This was news to me.

'Yes, Greece,' She nodded. 'You know, sunshine, retsina, bazouki music, John Travolta, Olivia Newton John, Greece.'

I got the message. 'We can't go away now!' I laid down the law.

'We aren't, I am.' Sarah answered with a smug little smile.

'Alone?'

'Of course not,' she informed me with a laugh, taking off the sarong and folding it neatly into a tiny rectangle.

'I see! Who are you going with? Some sugar daddy? Some father substitute? ' I asked suspiciously, already furious.

'Don't be so silly, Alan, 'she said in an aggrieved voice. 'I'm going with Beatrice.'

'Then she'll understand if you cancel. After all, she's a political animal,' I said, calming down. 'Now, there's a village show in Monkston on Sunday. . . .'

'I hope you enjoy it,' Sarah said unconcernedly. 'Beatrice and I are flying out on Saturday.'

'You can't. You mustn't! You're my wife! She's my agent! I'm facing a crisis! ' I protested in alarm. 'Don't either of you care about my political future? ' I asked her, scattering her dumb carrier bags with a kick.

'I can't speak for Beatrice,' Sarah said seriously as she picked up her plastic bags, 'But frankly, my dear, I don't give a damn.'

I stormed downstairs and rang Beatrice to give her a piece of my mind. How the hell could she piss off to Greece with my wife during my hour of need?

'Another fine mess you've got me into, Beatrice,' I told her off for slandering me to my father-in-law and causing this whole ruckus. Beatrice declared she was really glad I was finally going to get my come-uppance and hung up the phone on me with a cheery laugh, the cow. Then I rang Norman and arranged to meet him as soon as possible.

Norman had been evicted from his church in Parsons Green by a group of local vigilantes who called themselves Neighbourhood Watch. They'd accused him of being a Satan worshipper cum bag lady and had thrown him and his possessions out into the street in the middle of the night. At six o'clock the next morning, a passing kosher butcher, who was on his way back from the abbatoir, had taken pity on him, heaved all of his gear into his van and spirited him off to his shop in Temple Fortune, saying he couldn't stand the thought of a nice-looking lady like him being forced to walk the streets.

Norman had set up his office among the rows of meat hanging on hooks in the butcher's cold room. He was swathed in furs, including a fur hat which made him look not unsimilar to Gloria Swanson in *Sunset Boulevard*.

'Here's your visitor, miss', the butcher said to Norman as he ushered me into the cold room.

'You're taller than me,' the butcher addressed me. 'Do me a favour and reach down that chicken, will you?'

I reluctantly unhooked a chicken and handed it to the butcher who left the room, slamming the heavy metal door behind him.

'Why here, Norman? Christ, it's cold!' I said, stamping my feet.

'Don't mention Him in here. It's a kosher butcher,' Norman cautioned me in a whisper. 'Sit down.' He offered me a small blood-stained butcher's block to perch on.

'No, thank you,' I waved it away. 'I've got to keep moving. It's cold enough to freeze the balls off a brass pawnbroker!' I exclaimed as I moved from foot to foot quickly, flailing my arms around to get warm.

'Funnily enough, that's exactly why I wanted to see you,' Norman stated. 'I need ten thousand pounds to pay for the final and irrevocable step on the road from Norman to Norma.'

'Ten thousand pounds!' I exclaimed. Hardly a snip at the price.

Norman adjusted his hat to a more seductive angle, explaining, 'Private medicine is very expensive, and the operation I want isn't a health service cut. . . .'

'Norman, I've got more important things on my mind just now than laying out five Archers to have you streamlined,' I said wearily, impatient at his silly priorities.

'But you always promised you'd pay! I'm desperate, Alan!' he pleaded, his eyes twinkling with unshed tears, 'I can't go through life half man, half woman, I don't want to be in show business!'

The butcher came back into the cramped cold room to get down a side of beef. I moved toward the open door to catch a blast of warm air, promising, 'All right, all right. I'll give you the money if you come up with a way to save my political bacon.'

The butcher swept past me, glaring at me disapprovingly as I reached the word 'bacon'.

'The ball's in your court,' I challenged Norman with a shiver and followed the butcher out of the room.

I sat in my office, studying the current edition of *Whittaker's Almanac*, which I'd induced Piers to get me from the library. I had to find just the right charity to represent so as to make a big public splash quickly.

I phoned Bob Geldof, but Fifi Trixiebelle put the phone down on me. Then I tried AIDS Research, but an answerphone message said 'it only takes one litle prick to give you AIDS', so I rang off as I obviously wasn't the man for them. I next tried the Condom Commission, but they had just gone bust. Some time later I called Save the Children, but they were giving me a hard time.

'But I'm prepared to make a donation of fifty thousand pounds!' I repeated to the snooty Sloane on the other end of the line.

'No, only if you make me President,' I qualified my terms to the stupid girl. She asked me why. 'Because Save the Children is a charity close to my heart! Princess Anne's had a good run; it'll be a nice change her staying at home and ironing Mark Phillips's jodhpurs.'

The Sloane made some insulting remarks. 'In that case, I shall direct my largesse elsewhere,' I told her and hit the cradle of the receiver to disconnect the call. Consulting *Whittaker*'s again, I dialed another number.

'Hello. Yes, you can help me. I'm interested in becoming Master of the Corporation of Trinity House,' I stated and then told the weedy voice who asked me the reason for my strange request, 'Because I'm dedicated to the welfare of lighthouse keepers. No,' I repeated the little pervert's allegation, 'I am not attracted to sailors in general, and resent the implication.'

A knock on my office door interrupted my flow. A policeman stuck his head round the door. 'The Duke of Edinburgh? My God, they've got it all sewn up, haven't they?' I said when I was told in no uncertain terms who the Master already was. I hung up.

'Sorry to bother you, sir, but there's a lady out here says she has an appointment,' the policeman said, pointing into the corridor.

'What does she look like?' I frowned. I wasn't in the mood for unexpected visitors and their stupid little problems.

'Well, it's hard to say, sir,' the policeman equivocated, scratching his head. 'I suppose like someone out of Dallas.'

'Who? Sue Ellen?'

'Yes, Sue Ellen,' he agreed hesitantly, adding, 'With a touch of J.R.'

That could only be one person. And it was. The policeman admitted Norman, she was expertly made up and dolled up to the nines. She almost looked like a treat instead of a treatment, for once, I conceded. I now could believe she was a woman, but I still wasn't pleased to see her. She'd broken rule number one, and had come to see me in a public place.

'Thank you, constable,' I said politely as he left. I grimaced at Norman.

'What the hell are you doing out of cold storage?' I asked her when the coast was clear.

Norman said in her Fenella Fielding voice, 'I had to see you urgently!'

'All right, come over here,' I said, indicating my visitor's chair. She sat down and hitched up her skirt to show off her knees.

'Make it snappy,' I growled. 'I don't really want to be seen in the precincts of the Palace of Westminster with a transvestite.'

'I thought I looked rather good,' Norman said in a hurt voice.

'Yes, yes. You're gorgeous!' I snapped. 'Now get on with it!'

'You mean that? You're not just saying. . . .' she pouted and preened.

'Oh God. Yes, you're the most sublime creature that ever walked the earth,' I reassured her, to the sniggers of a passing MP.

'You don't think my calves are too muscly?' she asked in a tiresome girlish simper.

'Norman! Come to the point!' I urged. She was wasting my valuable time.

Norman removed her compact from her Gucci handbag, staring at her face in its little round mirror, she asked, 'Have you heard of Lamburger Guzzler?'

'Are you serious?' I sneered.

'Lamburger Guzzler is an American chain of fast food eateries.' She paused as she reapplied her lipstick and then pouted into the mirror, 'Their speciality is a one point seven five ounce lambmeat patty enhanced with nine secret spices and fourteen chemical additives,' she informed me.

'Yum yum. So?'

'So,' Norman announced, 'through my contacts in the meat trade, I've discovered they plan to open in Britain in a big way.'

'Oh, I see! I can campaign against them and become a hero!' I said, catching her drift.

'Quite the reverse, darling,' Norman drawled. 'They want to open two hundred Lamburger Guzzlers by the end of next year. That means they'll need a huge factory in a sheep-farming area of Britain, to supply them with zillions of patties; and, as you know, Haltemprice is a big sheep-rearing district. . . .'

'Is it?' I asked sheepishly. It was news to me.

'. . . so all you have to do is make sure that the factory is built in Haltemprice, and you'll be given the keys of the city,' she concluded triumphantly and stood up, adding, 'That will be ten grand.' She held out her hand.

'Hold on!' I said, scratching my chin in thought. 'There must be dozens of places they breed sheep, not including the Cabinet Room. Why should they come to Haltemprice?'

'Wouldn't you like to know?' She smiled coquettishly at me.

'Oh God, you're not going to play hard to get, are you?' I cried, totally fed up with Norman's flirtatious little mannerisms.

'I'll take a cheque,' Norman said bluntly. I got out my chequebook and started writing. She continued, 'If you take Regional Development Allowances into account, the Guzzler Corporation would be tossing millions away if they built anywhere other than Yorkshire. . . .'

'Really?' I said, tearing out Norman's payoff. 'That's excellent!'

'. . . or Wales,' Norman added.

'Oh. . . .'

'But it should be simplicity itself for a man of your talents to put Wales out of the running,' Norman challenged me.

'Probably,' I hedged as I thought rapidly. 'But I'm the one with the chequebook, so you tell me how.'

Norman reseated herself in a ladylike fashion and said, 'A cursory inspection of *The Wall Street Journal*'s directory of American millionaires would reveal that Willoughby Guzzler, father of the Lamburger, is a strict Christian fundamentalist. . . .'

The light dawned. 'Is he? In that case, it's my moral duty to ensure that Willoughby Guzzler discovers that Goronwy Hopkins, Secretary of State for Wales, is a notorious randy Welsh ram!'

'You've read my mind,' Norman smiled, lifting her well-plucked eyebrows at me.

'Norman, you're a genius!' I declared. 'If I didn't know your little secret, I'd kiss you. Here,' I said, handing her the cheque.

'Ten thousand. Thanks,' Norman said, examining the cheque. 'You haven't signed it!' she looked at me in accusation.

'Of course not,' I shrugged. 'I haven't finished with you yet. What are you doing tonight?' I asked, bracing myself for the shy little virgin's reaction to my startlingly simple plan.

If anyone was likely to have the dirt on Goronwy Hopkins, it was Sir Stephen, as they'd entered the House together in 1951.

I asked Sir Stephen if he'd introduce me to the Secretary of State for Wales as I was thinking of buying a holiday cottage in Gwent and wanted his advice. He agreed to perform this service that very evening and, as Goronwy is a Smoking Room regular, we went to have a few drinks and wait for him there.

I ordered a couple of double brandies and idly asked if Hopkins's notorious reputation for extra-curriculum activities was deserved.

'Oh yes, Goronwy Hopkins has always had a weakness for the fillies,' Sir Stephen nodded and sipped his brandy, adding, 'In fact, he was damned lucky his political career wasn't abruptly curtailed back in the Sixties.'

I transferred some brandy from my glass to his, demanding, 'Tell me more.'

'It was one of those sex scandals that periodically rock the Establishment,' Sir Stephen said delicately.

'Which scandal?' I asked incredulously.

'Do you know, I can't quite remember, there were so many in those days,' Sir Stephen said elusively. At my frown, he cleared his throat and recited, 'Goronwy was a Junior Minister and he developed a passion for some exotic dancer he met in a seedy nightclub. Then, one Friday, Goronwy developed a nasty cough and his doctor told him to spend the weekend in bed sucking a Fisherman's Friend. So he asked a close colleague, another Junior Minister, if he'd pop down to the nightclub in question and put the dancer off. Unfortunately, a freelance photographer for the *News of the World* happened to be in the club at the time. Well, Goronwy's colleague was ruined, and forced to resign from the Government . . . and I've been on the backbenches ever since,' he admitted ruefully.

'Ah, there he is, the thoroughly filthy fellow.' Sir Stephen looked at his ertswhile close colleague through narrowed eyes.

'Come on, Sir Stephen, you promised to introduce me, otherwise I wouldn't have bought you all those brandies,' I urged him, and he got up reluctantly to accompany me to the bar.

Sir Stephen greeted Goronwy with forced amity. 'Hopkins, good to see you. You're looking so well.'

The Minister of State for Wales turned to Sir Stephen and exclaimed, 'Baxter! Good Lord, man, I thought you'd been kicked upstairs years ago!'

Sir Stephen bristled, saying, 'No, still hanging on . . . on the backbenches.' Pointing his glass in my direction, he added, 'And this is my young protégé, Alan B'Stard. . . .'

'How do you do, sir?' I said. I shook his hand. 'It's a great honour to meet you. You must allow me to buy you a drink,' I offered genially.

'Allow you? Certainly, that's no hardship. Pint of best bitter,' he replied affably.

'Pint of best bitter and a large brandy,' I asked the bar man. Sir Stephen coughed to remind me of his presence. 'Do you sell Fisherman's Friends? No, then make it two brandies,' I amended the order.

Goronwy's eye was caught by a sexy-looking young female MP who was in conversation with a male colleague. 'Ooh, there's sexy, even if she is a Socialist! I wouldn't mind being liberal with her!' he said with a twinkle in his eye, and knocked back half of his pint in one go.

I nudged Sir Stephen, who said, 'B'Stard here is particularly interested in Welsh affairs. . . .'

Goronwy interrupted him, guffawing, 'I've had a few of those in my time, before the arteries hardened and the other thing softened. . . .'

'What was the exotic dancer's name?' Sir Stephen asked meanly. I slipped him a tenner to get lost. Expertly pocketing it, he said, 'Well, must be toddling along. Meeting an old Army chum at my Gentlemen's Club.' He stressed the word 'Gentlemen's' pointedly for Goronwy's benefit, and off he toddled.

'I thought the way you dealt with the Clwyd Reservoir Bill the other day was an example to us all,' I complimented Goronwy. Taking out a couple of aluminium tubes from my breast pocket, I offered one to him, 'Cigar?'

Goronwy took the cigar, saying, 'You mustn't tempt me. My old heart's not what it was. I shouldn't really be drinking.' He drained his glass and ordered the same again for himself and me from the bar man. 'Now what's a young go-getter like you doing sucking up to an old Druid in the autumn of his political career?' he asked with a laugh.

I shrugged and answered, 'It's simply that I have Wales in my blood.'

'There's a variation on the Jonah theme,' Goronwy smiled at his own feeble joke.

'You see, the name B'Stard signifies that I'm descended from James, Duke of Monmouth, the illegitimate son of Charles the Second. And, if he'd played his cards right back in 1685, you'd have been having a pint with King Alan,' I impressed him, exaggerating considerably.

Goronwy bowed and said, 'I am honoured.' Then his eyes lit up at a very attractive female Tory Junior Minister who had just come up to the bar. 'Look at the portfolio on that one! She can lean on my dispatch box any day,' he nudged me and whispered loudly.

'You're an admirer of the female form, aren't you?' I observed, finishing off my drink.

'Admirer? Worshipper, boyo,' Goronwy admitted proudly.

'Then you must come for a drink at my club,' I said, putting my empty glass down on the bar. 'There are some very friendly hostesses there.'

'Ooh, a bit naughty, are they?' he asked excitedly.

'Yes, a bit naughty, like Antarctica's a bit chilly,' I said to tempt him even more.

Hopkins downed the rest of his ale, saying, 'Hold on. I'll just get my anorak!'

We caught a cab to a sleazy basement club of my casual acquaintance in Shepherd's Market. It's called the Briefcase Club, maybe because its clientele all risk suffering from a brief case of the clap.

The club was dimly lit and littered with desperate and anonymous-looking middle-aged businessmen sitting with sexily dressed 'hostesses' who were plying them with watered-down champagne.

We went up to the bar. Goronwy ogled the tarts as I said to the blowsy barmaid, 'Bottle of champagne . . . the real stuff, not the Peardrax.'

The barmaid popped the cork of the bubbly as I excused myself to Goronwy, 'I've just got to pop to the cloaks.'

I made my way towards the Gents, searching for Norman. Eventually she emerged from the shadows and walked over to me in a beautiful, sexy, low-cut sequinned dress. She'd really pulled out all the stops, I had to grant her, but she appeared to be having a bad case of nerves, or was it PMT?'

'Alan, I don't like this,' she complained in a whisper, chewing on a long red fingernail.

'Ten thousand po-ounds!' I crooned as I dangled a hotel room key in front of her nose.

Norman stopped chomping and surveyed her manicure, which still passed muster. She slipped the key down the front of her dress into her bra and sashayed over to Goronwy. Perching on the stool next to him, she favoured him with a dazzling and seductive smile.

'Would you join me in a glass of bubbly, my dear? I hate drinking alone,' Goronwy asked, hooked, as he placed his hand on Norman's knee.

I slipped out of the club, collected my new autofocus camera from the Bentley and installed myself in the tacky hotel bedroom I'd booked for Norman and Goronwy's tryst.

Just for a joke, I also took my Ronald Reagan mask, which I put on as soon as I heard Norman and Goronwy approaching the hotel bedroom door. I crept into the wardrobe with my camera, leaving the door slightly ajar so that I could observe the action.

Norman unlocked the door and entered, followed by her swain, who was clutching a full bottle of champagne and two fluted glasses.

While Goronwy busied himself opening the champagne, Norman arranged herself seductively on the bed, with a little grimace at the wardrobe.

'I don't normally go into hotel rooms with strange men,' she trilled demurely.

'Neither do I!' Goronwy laughed, thinking he'd cracked a splendid joke. He filled the glasses and handed one to Norman. 'Here's to you, my dear,' he toasted her, taking a sip of champagne. He put the glass down on the bedside table and fell to his knees. He took Norman's hand and kissed it, saying, 'You really are an exceptional person, Norma. You combine a gorgeous feminine figure with a sharp, witty, dare I say masculine, mind.'

'You Welsh flatterer,' Norman said, putting her hand on her breast and batting her eyelashes at him.

'I mean it,' Goronwy averred, seating himself on the bed next to Norman and starting to run his hands al over her dress, murmuring, 'Your breasts are so firm.'

'They should be, I've only had them a few months. . . .' Norman said jestingly, as she tried to bat his hands away.

'What a sense of humour!' Goronwy panted as he continued to paw her, slipping his hand up the skirt of her dress.

'Please don't!' Norman shrieked, attempting to sit up and closing her legs together tightly.

'I know you girls. When you say no, you just want us boys to try harder!' Goronwy exclaimed, trying a great deal harder.

'No I don't!' Norman protested anxiously, but Goronwy managed to slide his hand even further up her dress.

'Relax, my dear, I'm a man of the world. I doubt you've anything up there I haven't come across before,' he comforted her.

'You want to bet?' Norman said as her assailant's hand reached her family jewels. Goronwy's face was a scream.

I leaped out of the wardrobe and started taking flash photographs of the sordid scene. Goronwy let out a startled oath in Welsh and slumped, a silent dead weight, on top of Norman, who struggled to get out from beneath him, crying, 'Goronwy???' and shaking him. She stood up and felt for his pulse, shaking her head at me. Reaching into her handbag, she got out her compact and flicked it open in front of Goronwy's mouth. There was no mist on the mirror.

'Save your flashbulbs, Alan. He's dead,' Norman said in a shocked voice.

I took off my mask to get a better look, saying, 'Is he? I think you're right.' I glanced at his trouser region and added, 'And it looks as if rigor mortis has already set in!'

I had the film developed within half an hour and had a dozen prints made of each shot. Then I went home and phoned a messenger service to take them immediately to Fleet Street and Wapping.

I managed to net twice the cost of Norman's final operation out of the proceeds from sales of the photos, so I wasn't too outraged by her final demand for a fortnight's pre-op holiday in Switzerland to get over the shock of her sudden over-exposure in the press.

I was delighted with *The Telegraph*'s treatment of the story: 'Silver-tongued Welsh Orator Comes To Sticky End In Arms Of Beauty Queen' was its page one lead story, although they'd used only one of my pix. *The Sun* was even better, blaring, 'Welsh Minister Dies On Job', with one of my most candid exposures blown up on page one and three more of my photos inside.

I was admiring my cuttings and scribbling a covering letter to Mr Willoughby Guzzler when Roland arrived in answer to my telephone call to him twenty minutes earlier.

'Roland, how very kind of you to call at such short notice,' I said warmly, opening the door to him graciously and leading him into my drawing room. 'Scotch? Havana?' I offered, ever the assiduous host.

'Yes, large, both,' he said abruptly, sweeping my cuttings on to the floor and usurping my favourite armchair for his own corpulent frame.

I filled Roland's order from my tantalus and the humidor, saying offhandedly, 'Terrible stink about old Goronwy Hopkins, eh? I don't suppose his local party were too pleased about his dying in the arms of a tart!'

'On the other hand, better to shaft a tart than your entire electorate!' the bastard countered, leafing through my cuttings.

'Then you haven't changed your mind about getting rid of

me?' I asked flatly as I handed the sod his drink and cigar.

'Certainly not!' Roland said emphatically. 'I thought you'd invited me here to accept your resignation in person.'

'Resign?' I asked lightly. 'When there's a vacancy at the Welsh Office?'

Roland leaned back in my armchair and lit his cigar, offering, 'You'd save yourself a great deal of damaging publicity if you did resign, instead of waiting to be sacked. You could always say you were quitting for personal reasons, to devote yourself to the accumulation of obscene wealth on a full-time basis.'

'No, Roland. I owe it to the executive council to appear before them and present my side of the case,' I said in a serious voice and sat down on the sofa, sipping my malt.

'Your case hasn't got a side!' Roland expostulated, thwacking the carpet with his walking stick in time to his words.

'If that's the decision of the council, then I shall of course abide by it,' I said staunchly, bluffing.

'You won't have any choice!' he shouted at me, with an accompanying thump of his stick.

I noticed his glass was already empty and got up to refill it, asking innocently, 'Trouble is, what would I do if I did have to resign?'

'I could make a suggestion, but you'd have to be double-jointed!' he sneered at me and lifted his freshened drink to his lips.

'I've been thinking about sheep-farming. . . .' I offered, returning to the sofa.

'Sheep?'

'Sheep; woolly beasts, trusting faces,' I started to clarify the word.

'I know about sheep!' Roland shouted, cutting me off. 'Been rearing the damned things for fifty years; though why I bother, with prices plummeting and those damn Froggie farmers hi-jacking our lorries. . . .'

'Does that mean you're selling up?' I asked innocently.

'I didn't say that,' Roland said guardedly.

'Just wondered,' I hinted casually, collecting my cutting from the floor and neatly folding my note. 'I don't mind paying a little above the market price for good beasts. . . .'

'How much above the market price?' he asked in a very interested manner.

'Let's wait until after the executive council meeting, shall we?' I stalled him as I sealed the cuttings and the letter into an envelope I'd already addressed and stamped. 'Now, if you'd be kind enough to drop this in a pillar box for me on your way home?' I asked, sensing the upper hand might be within my grasp once again.

'Oh, am I going?' Roland asked in an affronted tone, collecting his walking stick from the floor.

'Yes, I think so,' I said judiciously. 'After all, we don't actually like each other, do we?'

He drained his glass and I handed him the envelope. He peered at it, saying, 'Willoughby Guzzler, what an absurd name!'

'He's an American,' I explained.

'That's no excuse,' Roland snorted as I escorted him politely to my front door.

A week later, Willoughby Guzzler phoned me and said he'd just arrived in London and wanted to meet me as soon as possible. I arranged an appointment for four o'clock that same afternoon and he was bang on time.

Guzzler's police escort was dwarfed by his massive bulk, which was encased in one of those excrutiatingly loud plaid drip-dry suits Americans seem to favour. He also wore a ridiculous-looking leather thong tie, held in place round his jowly neck by a large silver sheep's head with glittering turquoise eyes. On his head was a ten-gallon hat which scarcely fitted through the doorway and on his feet were pointed high-heeled cowboy boots. All in all, he looked like the horse's arse he undoubtedly was.

'Mr Guzzler, how do you do?' I asked politely, dismissing the policeman and ushering Guzzler into my office. I extended my hand, which he took in his huge paw and pumped with bone-crunching vigour.

'I do just dandy, Mr Beestard,' he replied, adding, 'Do you mind if I call you Al?'

'Please do . . . Willoughby,' I winced internally but responded pleasantly.

'This is one hell of a classy office you have here, Al,' Guzzler said as he seated himself on my visitor's chair and slapped his knee.

'Thank you, though it's not simply an office block, it's also Parliament,' I remarked drily as I sat down behind my desk.

'I know that, Al,' Guzzler protested loudly. 'Gee whizz, soon as you Limeys hear a good old Southern drawl, you think you're dealing with some dumb-ass shit-kicker! Well, let me remind you, I have built up, in ten short years, the fifth biggest fast food business in the USA, and I'm here, out of the goodness of my heart, to bring my eateries to your shopping malls, jobs to your unemployed young folk, and wholesome lamburgers to feed your starving Northerners! So, let's not get off on the wrong cowboy boot, son!'

'Absolutely. Point taken!' I said quickly, taken aback, and mentally revised my tack, 'By the way, did you get those press cuttings I sent you about the late Goronwy Hopkins?'

'Sure did,' Guzzler nodded, a severe expression on his face. 'Terrible business, a government minister dying in such an undignified way.'

'What can you expect?' I said dismissively. 'The Welsh are essentially a pagan race, only drawn to Christianity by the opportunity for a good sing-song.' I took a deep breath and added more loudly, 'That's why only my God-fearing Yorkshire men. . . .'

'Hold your sheep, Al!' Guzzler exclaimed, raising his hand to stop me in mid-flow, 'I've just touched down, and I'm still jet-lagged. We'll have dinner together tomorrow night and that's when we'll talk turkey.' He ordered with a laugh.

'I'd rather talk lamburgers,' I jested.

'We will, Al, be sure of that,' he assured me with a broad smile, adding, 'And my little Edie is really eager to meet you and your good lady.'

'Good lady? You mean my wife?' I asked in moderate alarm.

'You are married, aren't you?' Guzzler frowned.

'Of course, very happily,' I replied heartily.

'Great, because we're a family business,' he said, rising and clapping me on the back. 'As Edie says, "The family that stays together, stays together." We make lousy mottoes but great burgers,' he chuckled.

'In that case, I'll just call my beloved and make sure she hasn't made any plans for tomorrow night,' I said as I tapped out the number.

Thankfully I got through on the second ring. 'Hello, Norma,' I said and told her of our forthcoming dinner date.

Once again, Norman more than came up to scratch, wearing a beautifully cut and very demure little black dress and pearls. I was wearing my best suit. Unfortunately, we were both a trifle overdressed for the occasion as Willoughby Guzzler's choice of restaurant was, in fact, his first British outpost in the Tottenham Court Road.

Guzzler was attired in an even louder suit than the one he'd worn the previous day. His blowsy Dolly Parton-ish wife was wearing jeans, a cowgirl shirt, masses of diamonds and a super-abundance of make-up.

They queued at the counter to collect our vittles, while I sat with Norman at the formica table, pining in vain for a malt whisky and listening to Norman's endless complaints.

'I don't believe you're ever going to send me to Switzerland. You're just using me!' Norman accused me for the third time in two minutes.

I handed her an envelope containing the wretched certified cheque, saying, 'Calm down, here's your cheque. You didn't think I'd keep you dangling forever?' I quipped.

Norman ripped open the envelope in delight and planted a big kiss on my cheek, which I had to suffer with a smile as Willoughby and Edie arrived back at the table with our so-called food.

'You can see he loves her nearly as much as we love lamburgers, Edie,' Willoughby remarked to his wife as they distributed four large cheese 'n lamburgers, four giant-sized portions of fries and four outsized thick chocolate milkshakes round the table. As Edie set the table with plastic cutlery and paper napkins, Willoughby sat down and said, 'All the food for this outlet is airlifted in from Virginia, but when we start expanding. . . .'

'You'll need Yorkshire sheep,' I finished his sentence for him eagerly.

'Could be, Al,' Willoughby said agreeably. 'Well, eat up, everyone, while they're hot and greasy.'

Willoughby and Edie tucked in as I recited piously, 'For what we are about to receive, may the Lord make us truly thankful. Amen.'

I took a bite of my burger. 'It's quite pleasant,' I said in surprise.

'It should be, it's one hundred per cent farm-raised lamb,' Willoughby nodded his head vigorously, continuing, 'What do you say, Norma?'

'I just feel so overdressed,' Norman replied, pouting at him.

'No way, I think you look cute!' he said, with a wink at her.

I was really starting to enjoy my lamburger. 'So, it's actually pure meat, is it?' I asked.

'Depends on what you mean by meat. You see, we have a no-waste policy. Bones, brains, balls, everything goes into the mincer,' Willoughby explained through a mouthful of fries. 'By the time we've finished with the sheep all that's left is the little bell that used to hang round the poor varmint's neck.'

'Very efficient,' I commented, suddenly having difficulty in swallowing my meat. I took a long suck at the straw of my shake, which was nearly an impossible operation as the shake proved thicker than Piers Fletcher-Dervish. 'So, tell me, Willoughby, how many sheep will you need to slaughter per annum in England?' I asked, getting down to the business at hand.

'Depends on turnover,' Willoughby shrugged and turned to his wife. 'What do you say, Edie?'

'Well, we average sixty-seven carcases per week per outlet. At an average of forty-three pounds of useable sheep-product per carcase, times two hundred eateries,' Edie calculated aloud.

'That's nearly six million lamburgers!' Norman trilled excitedly.

'Five million, seven hundred and sixty-two thousand, to be precise,' Edie drawled, wiping her mouth daintily on a paper napkin.

'Looks like both our gals got brains as well as beauty,' Willoughby said, nodding at me approvingly.

'Thank you, Willoughby,' Norman accepted the compliment with aplomb, finishing her fries with her knife and fork.

'Yes, I think we can both thank the Lord we've been so blessed in our choice of helpmates. In fact, I feel like dropping to my knees and giving thanks right here and now!' I said and knelt down on the lino in a prayerful attitude.

'And dames who are smart in the office are usually smart in the sack, huh, Edie?' Willoughby nudged his wife and laughed lewdly. I couldn't believe my ears.

'I've never had any complaints, Willow,' Edie said in a sexy tone and tickled her husband under one of his chins, adding, 'From you or anyone else. How about you, Norma?'

I reclaimed my seat, more than a little confused by the turn the conversation was taking. 'Norma's a one-man woman,' I announced.

'In every imaginable way!' she tittered nervously and frowned at me in dismay.

I tried to change the subject with, 'Willoughby, you must come up to Haltemprice as my guest, see the beautiful farms, the very impressive industrial development sites. . . .'

'Yeah, okay,' Willoughby tapped me on the shoulder to shut me up and continued, 'You mean to say, Norma, that you've never screwed around?'

'That's a very personal question,' Norman said demurely, lowering her eyes to her lap.

'What about you, big boy?' Edie cosied up to me and breathed into my ear. 'Do you swing?'

'I belong to a couple of golf clubs,' I attempted a joke.

'I just love your British sense of humour, it's so sexy,' she said, drawing her sharp fingernails down the front of my shirt.

'Why don't we all go back to our hotel suite? There's a jacuzzi, a water bed, we've bought a pile of stag movies with us from the States,' Willoughby suggested loudly and lewdly. He caught Norman's hand and said, 'If you loosen up, honey, we can really party!'

'I'm a married woman!' Norman grabbed her hand back. Reluctantly I put my arm about her protectively.

Edie made a little moue at me and said, 'I'm a married woman too. I wouldn't dream of cheating on my Willow. I always tell him when I'm about to swing with another guy. . . .'

'And if I'm videoing it, she can hardly be accused of going behind my back, can she?' her Willow laughed and drained his shake noisily.

'I suppose not,' I said hesitantly. Then, taking a deep breath and deciding in for a penny, in for a pound, I declared, 'Willoughby, I have to say I'm rather shocked by this conversation. I mean, I thought you were a deeply devout and committed Christian!'

'Me? Sheeyit, no!' he laughed raucously. 'You must be mixing me up with my pappy, Willoughby Guzzler the Second. He's a real tight-ass Jesus freak! But me, why, I just live for today, and let the devil take the hindmost!' he announced, putting his arm round Norman's waist. 'Come on, baby, like it says in the song, I'm as horny as Kansas in August!'

Norman clung to me in alarm, whispering, 'Alan, I couldn't go through that again!'

I actually fancied a roll in the hay with Edie quite a lot, but of course I couldn't risk allowing Willoughby access to Norman's little secret. 'I'm sorry, Mr Guzzler, I'm sure your invitation for us to come back to your hotel and "party" was well-meant, but Norma and I are sincere Christians, and the only sin we're interested in is the Synod of the Church of England,' I asserted self-righteously.

'Hallelujah!' Willoughby shouted triumphantly and dropped to his knees.

'What?' I asked, doubly confused.

'Hallelujah! Praise God!' Willoughby repeated and heaved himself to his feet, explaining, 'I am the deeply devout Willoughby Guzzler the Second! Edie and me, we've just been tempting you, like the Lamb of God was tempted in the desert. . . .'

'Lamb of God?' I asked Norman in a whisper.

'He means Jesus,' Norman explained to me behind her hand.

Willoughby and Edie shook us both by the hand as Willoughby apologised, 'I hope you'll both forgive me for the profanities I've uttered, but we had to be sure before I built my factory in your town. You see, just before he passed over, Goronwy

Hopkins sent me a long letter saying I shouldn't site my factory in Haltemprice, on account of the Member of Parliament being a real dirty dog!'

'Does that mean I get the factory?' I asked gleefully.

Willoughby nodded his confirmation. 'We'll sign the papers tomorrow, and before you know it we'll be turning over the sod. . . .'

Out of the corner of my mouth, I remarked to Norman, 'And I can't wait to see the sod's face when I tell him!'

A week later I had Haltemprice eating out of my hand and Roland Gidleigh-Park eating very humble pie.

We were standing in my drawing room. Roland had come to see his daughter, hoping I would be out. I poured myself a glass of malt whisky and lit a cigar, ostentatiously offering him neither.

'I don't know why you're so out of sorts, Roland. You wanted a vote of censure from the local party and you got one,' I remarked mildly.

Roland shouted, 'But they censured me!' and stamped his gamy foot on the floor, wincing with the pain.

'Naturally,' I was delighted to say. 'They could see that you'd been trying to victimise a successful and popular Member of Parliament, a man who has brought to Haltemprice a brand new factory that will employ two hundred people. A man who will bring added prosperity to dozens of farmers, their families and serfs. A man who has put this town on the map. . . .'

'Shut up! Shut up!' Roland ordered. 'I don't want to hear this.'

I smiled smugly and asked, 'Then why did you call?'

'You damn well know why! I want my sheep back! You bought them under false pretences!' he shouted.

'Not at all,' I took great pleasure in contradicting him. 'I told you I was prepared to pay above the going rate for sheep, and asked you to put the word around. Instead, you sold me your entire flock the next day, without letting anyone else in on the deal. You were a greedy old man.'

'All right, damn it!' Roland barked at me, puce in the face with fury. 'I'll buy them back at today's price.'

'I'm afraid that's not possible, Roland,' I told him truthfully. 'You see, they've all been slaughtered, butchered and are hanging in cold storage waiting for the lamburger factory to open.'

'You can't do that, you raving lunatic!' Roland cried. 'They were wool sheep!'

I shrugged and said, 'Doesn't matter when you're making lamburgers. It all goes through the mincer; bones, brains, balls . . . fleece. Staying for dinner? It's lamb chops. . . .' I smirked triumphantly as he slammed his way out of my home. Vengeance is mine saith the Commoner.

THE END